C000233393

BORN YESTERDAY

Also by Douglas Sutherland

BIOGRAPHY
The Yellow Earl: The 5th Earl of Lonsdale
Burgess and Maclean
The Fourth Man: Burgess, Maclean, Philby and Blunt
Twilight of the Swans: A life of Cosima Wagner
Fraud: The amazing career of Dr Emil Savundra
The Mad Hatters: Sporting Eccentrics of the 19th Century

MILITARY HISTORY
The Argyll and Sutherland Highlanders
Tried and Valiant: The History of the Border Regiment

AUTOBIOGRAPHY
Against the Wind: An Orkney Idyll
Rohallion
Sutherland's War

HUMOUR
The English Gentleman
The English Gentleman's Wife/Child/Mistress
The English Gentleman Abroad
The English Gentleman's Good Shooting Guide
The English Gentleman's Good Fishing Guide
The Art of Gentle Gardening

GENERAL
Behold! The Hebrides
The Landowners
Portrait of a Decade: London Life 1945–1955
Raise Your Glasses
The Salmon Book

FICTION
Strike!

BORN YESTERDAY

Memories of a Scottish Childhood

DOUGLAS SUTHERLAND

CANONGATE

First published in Great Britain in 1992 by
Canongate Press plc, 14 Frederick Street,
Edinburgh EH2 2HB

ISBN 0 86241 403 2

British Library Cataloguing-in-Publication Data
A catalogue record for this book is available on request from
the British Library.

Phototypeset by Falcon Typographic Art Ltd, Fife, Scotland
Printed and bound in Great Britain by Biddles Ltd, Guildford

For my late wife Diana and for my children
Carol, James, Adam, Charlie and Jo-Jo
who deserve some sort of explanation.

CHAPTER ONE

'Begin at the beginning' the King said, gravely 'and go on till you come to the end; then stop . . .'

Alice in Wonderland Lewis Carroll

I was born on the 18th November 1919 at Bongate Hall, Appleby, in the County of Westmoreland, the second of three sons in the family.

From this bald statement of the facts of my birth, it will be readily appreciated that I came into this world, disadvantaged in every possible way. In the first place 1919 was a sort of non-year. There is a certain prestige in being born a war baby and particularly of a war now so infinitely remote as the bloody conflict of 1914–18. To miss that distinction by exactly one year and one week was hard cheese indeed. At the same time I missed by a mere six weeks being a 1920s' baby which does not sound nearly so long ago and has all the overtones of an emancipated generation which had thrown off the shackles of Victorianism and was to erupt, at least for the socially privileged, in all the fizz and crackle which was to epitomise the 20s and 30s until yet another world war was to pull down the shutters again.

Perhaps worse than being born in a kind of limbo, was the geographical location which my parents had selected for this momentous event. Appleby is, to my mind, one of the most fetching of all the villages and townships which are scattered in such profusion in one of the most attractive corners of England but it fails, by a mere twenty-five miles as the crow flies, to be on the right side of the Scottish border. Thus I became the only one on both sides of my family, reaching back for uncounted generations, not to be able to boast proudly of being born and bred in Scotland.

What exactly my parents were up to, renting Bongate Hall over the winter of 1919 has never been properly explained to me. My father had been invalided out of the Gordon Highlanders, after being badly gassed at Passchendaele, and had first met my mother when he was recuperating at her family home, Kinloch, in Perthshire which had been turned into a home for wounded officers for the duration of the war. He, and his family for generations before him, came from the Orkney Islands where they owned quite a modest sized island. Further back in history there had been Norse blood but otherwise there had been no cross-pollination with any of Scotland's erstwhile enemies and certainly not with the English.

Bongate Hall, when I came to revisit it many years later, turned out to be, despite its rather grand description, quite one of the most spectacularly ugly houses one could imagine. It was a ramblingly pretentious, red brick Victorian nightmare which, in its declining years, had suffered the basest of all ignomies by being turned into a temperance hotel-cum-boarding-house. Mercifully, some ten years ago, it was put out of its agony and razed to the ground to make way for some rather super modern flats.

A further disadvantage from which I was to suffer all my life was my name. It is not that I am not proud of the name of Sutherland with its echoes of Scotland's turbulent past when we ruled that wild and lawless territory which occupies almost the whole of Scotland north of what is now the Caledonian Canal. What is wrong with the name in these more practical times is that it begins with 'S' and is therefore very far down in the batting order when applications for anything desirable are taken as is usual in alphabetical order. Those with a name like Aaron cannot know how lucky they are. And then again as a name it is far too long. To add to this injury my parents had me christened with the forenames of Douglas Chalmers Hutchinson. Try to fit this in, together with the name of Sutherland, on one of those forms which are becoming increasingly prevalent, in the tiny space provided and it will be readily appreciated what the Fates have lumbered me with.

And then, of course, there is the matter of being a second son in a world where the eldest, by right of primogeniture, inherits the earth whilst the youngest, by tradition, is pampered and adulated beyond all reason. Second sons are, by and large, expendable.

Whatever prompted my parents to camp for a time at Bongate Hall, it was not to last for very long. My first childhood memory is of an incident which remains brilliantly illuminated after all these years. It occurred, so I was later told, when the train which was taking the family north drew into Stirling railway station. In those days it was the habit, if not the rule, that the Station Master met trains stopping at his station wearing an immaculately polished top hat and cut-away tail coat. Thus attired he would greet passengers alighting from the train (first class passengers only, I suspect) when a particularly deep bow might earn him a handsome tip. In those long ago days when the nationalisation of the railways was still in the far distant future, the gentry owned the railways either by being shareholders or on account of the railway passing through their landed estates where, as often as not, they had their own private station built for the convenience of themselves and their guests.

On this occasion, the Station Master at Stirling had only just replaced his top hat as the train drew out of the station when a sudden gust of wind blew it off again and sent it bouncing along down the platform, revealing that the unfortunate man was as bald as a billiards ball!

I had up to this moment been, apparently, in a state of uncontrolled grief and bawling my head off ever since we had embarked on the journey. At the sight of this misfortune, however, I became in high good humour and continued to gurgle with delight for the remainder of the trip. As to that I cannot vouch but the sight of the bald Station Master chasing his top hat down the platform has remained forever green in my memory. For the rest, my memory remains nearly a complete blank until I was almost three years old.

The journey on which we had embarked was no ordinary one, nor one to be lightly undertaken by a child of less than a year old. We, with my elder brother Gordon, were travelling north to my father's home on Stronsay, one of the smaller and more remote of the Orkney Islands where he and my mother were to start their married life. Stronsay is a straggly sort of island which measures no more than seven miles from tip to furthest tip. Father's house was on a narrow neck of land, joining the west limb of the island to the main body. On one side were the often treacherous waters of the North Sea and on the other the majestic rollers of the Atlantic Ocean beat in upon a great expanse of sandy beach.

In my grandfather's day there had only been a small croft there where he had brought his wife and family of five sons during the summer holidays. For the rest of the year they occupied an imposing square-built house above Kirkwall, overlooking the bay, on Mainland which was the name given to the largest of the islands. Scotland, across the stormy waters of the Pentland Firth, was what the Orcadians like to describe, pawkily, as 'the adjacent island'.

Grandfather in his youth had, like so many of the islanders, set out to the far corners of the globe to make his fortune. He had arrived, with a fellow Orcadian, Bill Hutchinson, in South Africa just at the time when the great diamond and gold mining era was reaching its zenith. With Hutchinson (after whom I take one of my forenames) he formed a construction company which was carried along on the crest of the boom. Cecil Rhodes, the most powerful man in South Africa, took them under his wing and through him they got the contract, amongst other major developments, of building the Cape Town to Johannesburg railway line. They returned, passing rich certainly by Orkney standards, and each set up in some style in Kirkwall and each bought land on the outlying islands to serve as what I suppose nowadays might be described as 'holiday homes'.

My father was his eldest son who had gone to Edinburgh Unversity to study medicine. Then the Great War came along, during which Grandfather died and Dad had inherited the island. He gave up any idea of continuing his medical studies and decided to settle on the island and farm his lands there. His first thought was to convert the modest croft and its outbuildings into a suitable house for his young wife and growing family.

Father always had rather big ideas and the reconstruction of the old croft was an opportunity to give them full range. Expert stonemasons were imported to dress the blocks of red sandstone hewn from the island quarry and elaborate gardens were laid out, surrounded by a fine stone wall. By island standards a garden on this scale was considered a luxury indeed.

Because of the violent gales which sweep the islands any attempt to grow flowers could only be successful in the most sheltered positions. To achieve this he had deep holes dug into the lawns and filled them with various plants and shrubs. Thus the garden consisted of a series of rose-holes, tulip holes and so on. I don't think this ever proved to be a great success but it added to the wonder of the islanders at these strange goings-on.

There was another problem to be faced which was that the island, like all the Orkneys, is devoid of trees. Thus all the wood had to be imported and, with the wood, came a tribe of carpenters who lived in tents on the site whilst they worked on the pannelled interior of the house as well as building other facilities such as, of all things, a garage. This was an intriguing innovation for the islanders, many of whom had never even seen a car. As a final touch, Father had his coat of arms carved in stone above the front door which itself was made from a great single slab of heavily studded oak which would have done credit to a medieval castle.

Father, I think, felt that he had some sort of potential as an architect and designed the interior of the house which was all built on one floor. There was a large (to my childish eyes) central hall off which ran what seemed to be endless corridors. It was probably due to Father's inexperience that none of the corridors were quite on the level. The result was that, in what was rather grandly called the nursery wing, the night nursery was on a considerably higher level than the day nursery, so that my brother and I could quite easily slide down it on a tea tray.

When all was done and finished, he named the house Mountpleasant and settled down to the life of an Orkney laird.

CHAPTER TWO

Long time he lay upon the sunny hill,
To his father's house securely bound.
Far off the silent, changing sound was still,
With the black islands lying thick around.

He saw each separate height, each vaguer hue,
Where the massed islands rolled in mist away,
Though all ran together in his view
He knew that unseen straits between them lay.

Childhood Edwin Muir

My earliest memories of the island are of the wind. During the long winter months the wind ruled our lives. A day without wind was something to be remarked on but the great gales when they started to blow were something quite different. Then the whole island would seem to flatten out, lashed by tall plumes of spray so that land and sea became almost indistinguishable and the booming of the waves as they hit the high cliffs at Lamb's Head filled the air with clamorous noise. Sometimes a gale might last several days and then blow itself out quite suddenly, leaving an impression of sudden calm save for the angry roaring of the sea.

When the gale is at its most fierce it comes in shuddering gusts as if some giant were pausing to draw in his breath only to gather strength to blow again all the harder. For my brother Gordon and me the gales were a time of high excitement. There is an extraordinary exhilaration in the sounds of a storm when you are safely barricaded against it. It sharpens the senses so that the simplest action, such as crossing a room, becomes charged with drama. When an extra strong gust came, the whole house seemed to flinch and the paraffin lamp swayed on its hook on the ceiling so that the shadows danced on the wall and gave the feeling that everything was moving, as if on a ship.

It was an excitement not shared by our mother. For her the storms were a time of unseen danger. To our great delight we were allowed to have our supper in the grown-ups' sitting room, crouched in our dressing gowns round the peat fire when our mother would cuddle us to her as if to protect us from all the demons and furies let loose in the night. For our father, inured as he had been from boyhood to the force of the equinoctial gales, it was still a time of heightened anxiety. Because of the wind everything that could be moved had to be tied down. A piece of farm equipment left carelessly lying about, a load of hay not safely stowed away in a barn or even livestock left to the mercy of the storm would be picked up as if by a giant hand and whirled away never, in all likelihood, to be seen again.

There is one storm in particular which is part of my very earliest memories. We were all gathered round the fire whilst outside the wind shrieked with what seemed to be more than usual malevolence. Father started fidgeting, lighting one cigarette after another and generally showing all the signs of getting into a high old state. Finally he could stand it no longer.

'It's that damned henhouse we got last week' he said. 'I'm not sure I have got it properly anchored down.'

'Well it's too late to do anything about it now' my mother said rather snappishly but that seemed to make the nervous symptoms even worse. Finally he declared that he would he would just 'take a wee look'.

This brought a further vigorous protest from Mum, convinced that he would be swept away and what would we all do then, left fatherless in a cruel world? Unmoved he plunged out across the yard and came back to report that the pickets were showing signs of lifting and that the hens would have to be evacuated to the safety of the house. It took six journeys to bring them all in to sit blinking and dishevelled in the kitchen. Only the cock took evasive action to avoid capture, so he was left to the last in the true tradition of the captain of his ship. As Father stood poised to make a final dash across the yard he saw by the light from the kitchen window, the whole hen house lifted into the air and, turning over and over, disappear into the darkness.

When I awoke the next morning, the first thing which filtered through to me was the silence and, peering out from under the bedclothes, I could see the watery sunlight shafting through the cracks in the storm shutters. The contrast from the night before was so great that it was some time before I was conscious of the angry roaring of the sea. Even then it did not affect the quality of the silence which had settled so deeply on the house that it made even the dripping of the bathroom tap sound unnaturally loud.

Without even waiting to dress we hurried out in our night clothes to gaze in awe at the mountainous seas. Where the hen house had been there was now only a jagged scar in the earth where the pickets which held the wire strapping the henhouse to the ground, had pulled out. Then we caught sight of what had been left of the hen house. It had been blown fully two hundred yards up the road and now lay, a mass of broken boards and twisted roofing felt, against a stone dyke which had stopped it crashing into the sea. Perched on the very topmost spar, arrogantly flapping his bedraggled wings was the gallant cock. As we watched, he threw back his head and crowed defiance to a watery world. Even at the age of four, it struck me as being an inspiriting moment.

Après-storm was always the most exciting time on the island and the times I can remember most clearly. As soon as the wind had died away we would hurry down to the long sandy beach on the Atlantic side of the island. To walk along the sand above the high-water mark was to walk into a world of wonder. Every few yards we would come upon an incredible variety of fish which had been hurled up out of the sea. There would be great triangular skate with their long whip-like tails, quantities of halibut and cod, their vacant-looking eyes glazing over in death. Sometimes there would even be small sharks who would lie there for weeks until the birds had picked their bones clean and the tiny chubby pilot fish, the close escorts of the predatory sharks so that they could feed off the remnants of their victims. We would carry our share of the beached white fish back to the house in triumph to be cooked for lunch the following day.

There were also always quantities of driftwood, scrubbed white by the sea and, on one occasion, slabs of cork which were to serve us as bathroom mats for many years to come. On the North Sea side, which was rocky and covered in seaweed, there were exciting pools to explore. For the most part they only held some of the many varieties of crab and occasionally some small fish left behind by the tide. The greatest triumph was to capture a lobster. Left behind by the retreating tide, the lobsters would seek a refuge under the rocks where the sea had hollowed out tiny caves. The technique was to prod a stick warily into the hole. If there was a lobster in residence, it would be enraged at having its privacy thus invaded and would sieze the stick in its powerful claws and hang on whilst it was dragged out of its refuge and grabbed by the back to be dropped into a basket. I don't think I ever caught a lobster in this way being rather too young to get involved in such a dangerous business. If a lobster gets a hold on a careless finger, it will hang on literally to the death.

Our constant companion on these expeditions was our nurse-governess, Miss Johnstone. She had been in charge of us ever since I could remember. Although life on the island was very restrictive from a social point of view, Mother and Father were always rather remote figures in our lives. Mamma, once we had got out of bed and were washed and breakfasted, liked to take us riding if the weather was fine, handing us back to Miss Johnstone to be washed all over again before nursery lunch which would be probably the last we would see of either parent until it was time to go through in our pyjamas and dressing gowns to the drawing room to say good-night.

Miss Johnstone was a perfectly splendid person. She had

been an Olympic high diving champion and was in her element in water. The sea in those northerly climes was never, it seemed to me when venturing to put a toe in it, very much above freezing point. This made not the slightest difference to Miss Johnstone. Come what may she would have her morning swim. I can see her now, far out in the bay, her white bathing cap bobbing in the waves and sometimes disappearing entirely in the troughs. When she emerged, like some Aphrodite rising from the foam, she would towel herself vigorously and race up and down the beach with us on our Shetland ponies.

Walks with Miss Johnstone (although I loved her to death I never got to know her first name) were of an equally vigorous character. We did not really walk. We marched, often to the sound of snatches off suitable songs. As we passed the cemetery, for example, Miss Johnstone would strike up with 'John Brown's body lies a-mouldering in the grave, while His soul goes marching on!' Other favourites were 'It's a long, long way to Tipperary' or, if we looked like flagging, 'Keep right on the the end of the road, keep right on to the end.'

It was on one of those rare occasions when Gordon and I could go off on our own for walks that we came by the greatest and most exciting discovery of all. Unsupervised walks were altogether a different matter from the route marches which we, quite happily, endured with Miss Johnstone. Let off the leash we would head for the sand dunes where we could slide down the high banks of sand and tumble about to our hearts' content. More daringly we would clamber out on what was generally believed to have been an old Pictish pier. Made out of flat stone slabs, set on their edges, they had endured for centuries. When the tide was high the end of the pier was almost under water, the slippery, seaweed-encrusted stones washed by the waves. A false step and one could fall into deep water – or, at least, out of our depth and like most island-bred children we had not yet learned how to swim.

We were just contemplating a perilous trip to the end of the pier and deciding who should go first, when at our feet, lying on the leeward side of the stones, was a baby seal gazing at us with its big, trusting doe eyes and an air more of languid curiosity than anything else. When we went to pick it up, it lay supine in our arms; a white fluffy bundle, showing only the mildest curiosity at this turn of events in its young life. Staggering under its considerable weight, we took it in turns to carry it home, keenly anticipating the warmth of our welcome at bringing back such a wonderful addition to the household. It is one of the sad facts of life that the keener the expectations, the less likely they are to be realised. It will suffice to say, therefore, that our reception when we finally arrived home fell very far short of being rapturous. When we appeared with our prize at the kitchen door Harriet Hourston, our cook, would, I believe, have slammed the door in our faces had she seen the baby seal in time. As it was she shrank from us as if we were some sort of manifestation of the Devil. We were only to learn later that there was a superstition amongst some of the islanders that upon death the spirit entered into a seal and went to lie out on the flat rocks with its ancestors. To have a seal in the house, like many other things in island mythology, was to bring ill-luck as certain as the rising and the setting of the sun.

Mother and Father's objections were of a rather more practical nature. Chief amongst them was the humanitarian one that, removed from its natural environment, it would certainly die, to which was added the rider that, if it did not die, it would only become the most dreadful nuisance about the place. Miss Johnstone, who was confined to her bed with one of her periodic migraines, was consulted and, to our great joy, came out firmly on our side. To be returned to the sea without being re-united with its mother from whom it had obviously become parted in the storm, would result in its certain death from starvation. This argument, added to our own wailings and lamentations, carried the day. Even Harriet Hourston was convinced that to allow it to die would cause offence in the spirit world and certainly no good would come of that. So converted was she that, from the beginning, it was allowed to live in the kitchen, where it slept for most of the day, lying outstreached on the stone flags, its flippers straight down by its side and its muzzle stretched out like an exhausted dog.

The decision that we could keep our baby seal at once raised the urgent question of how it was to be fed. Fortunately Miss Johnstone proved to be something of an authority, as she was on many other abstruse matters, on the bringing up of seals. As the milk of the mother seals was far richer than cows' milk, it was decreed that it should have the cream from the top of the milk pails to which, for good measure, cod liver oil should be added and fed from a baby's bottle. Our seal took to this diet with the greatest of enthusiasm whilst the rest of us subsisted without complaint on skimmed milk.

When it came to giving it a name, it seems that inspiration was sorely lacking. One impediment was that nobody had any idea of its sex nor any inkling of how this could be discovered. Thus it was that it was always referred to as Baby. A description that was, in a very short time, to become totally inappropriate.

Within a week Baby was proving Father's forecast of its nuisance value to be, if anything, an underestimation. Seals as a species are, by nature, filled with an overweening curiosity. If you come across them basking on the rocks, they will make a hasty dive for the water only to reappear again a few yards away to subject the intruder to the closest scrutiny. Baby indulged this characteristic by hauling itself across the kitchen floor poking its nose into everything, overturning the scrap bucket or the bread bin with the greatest regularity. Nor were its house manners, despite all our efforts, anything to write home about.

Soon the kitchen took on the air of being constantly under siege with everything moveable on the floor piled up in the table and shelves. Amazingly Harriet, her earlier forebodings forgotten, far from complaining about this state of affairs became almost slavishly devoted to Baby, clearing up all the mess with the greatest of good humour.

An even more surprising convert was Father. Soon he set himself up as the greatest living expert on the upbringing of baby seals and it was in this capacity that he decreed that it was time Baby had its first swimming lesson. It was no sooner said than done. The bath was filled almost to the brim and we were all paraded to watch the christening. Father himself lowered her (we were becoming increasingly persuaded from the capriciousness of her behaviour that Baby must be a she) into the water. No sooner did her extremities touch what should have been her natural element than she started to struggle for all the world like a panic-striken kitten afraid of getting its fur wet. When Father finally let go of her, her struggles became ever more furious, thrashing around and soaking everyone within range and getting more waterlogged by the second.

When, at the expense of his becoming completely drenched, Father rescued her from this undignified predicament, Baby eyed us all with such reproach that we came to the conclusion that we owned the only non-swimming seal in the world.

Baby, with her winning ways, took a step backwards in the popularity stakes with the next stage in her natural development. She started to shed her long white silky coat. This, coupled with a newly-acquired mobility, resulted in all the carpets in the corridors and any rooms to which she managed to gain access, being smothered in hairs. At the same time she started to acquire the dappled grey, short-haired coat of the adult seal, giving her a comical piebald appearance.

The time had come by a majority ruling (only my brother and I dissenting) for Baby to be banished from the house and for her to take up a new residence prepared for her in the hay barn. This was very far from her liking and soon she settled for sleeping underneath the motor car on the cement floor of the garage. From this point of vantage she would emerge at exactly eight o'clock in the morning when breakfast was being prepared and stage a demonstration outside the kitchen door until she was admitted. This took the form of making a sort of bleating noise, rather like a new-born lamb. Worse, and more sympathy-inducing, tears would pour down her cheeks in the most heart-rending fashion.

In fact the apparent ease with which seals burst into tears

has nothing to do with the state of their emotions. It is simply that, when on dry land, Nature has not fitted them with ducts to dispose of surplus eye liquid so that water flows down their cheeks in the most distressing way, giving the impression that they are totally overcome with grief.

Very soon Baby took to following any of us around, giving ecstatic grunts of pleasure whenever we appeared. Then she was following us down to the rocky beach when the tide was out and, her aversion to water forgotten, she played around happily in the large pools. Sometimes she would play football with us and at others simply float face downwards and inert with her head underwater as if dead. It was during one of these feigning dead moods that our attention was distracted by some new discovery or other. When next we looked at Baby, she was making all haste for the sea and was already too near to the edge for us to stop her. We stood, rooted to the spot as with one final joyous wriggle she plunged into the waves. A few moments later she was diving and frolicking far out in the bay. There was nothing we could do. Nor was it any solace when finally we abandoned hope and returned, tearfully, to the house to be told that it was 'all for the best' and the comfort offered by Harriet that she would now have been welcomed by her ancestors.

Next morning when we were sitting red-eyed and miserable at the breakfast table, there was a familiar commotion outside the back door and there she was looking eagerly for her bottle as if nothing had happened. After that she would make off on her own every day down to the sea and return each evening to sleep under the car. I think that we now accepted that when the breeding season came round in the Spring, she would finally go to join her own kind on the sea-girt holms and leave us forever. Sadly it was not to be.

One day when we were out with our ponies we came across her body, clubbed to death by some unknown hand. Whether her killer was motivated by some age-old superstition or purely from malevolence, we were never to know.

It is difficult to get the chronology right of one's early childhood and isolated memories run together like a kind of colour gouache. At this time I think I must have been in my third year, coming up to my fourth birthday in November. My brother, Gordon, was a year and five months my senior which gave me certain advantages of which I was, of course, not conscious at the time. Living as we did in almost total isolation, the nearest habitation being over a mile away and with only our legs to carry us there, we might have been twins so closely were our lives intertwined. Thus we learnt to read together as well as to do simple sums with a little painting and drawing thrown in. Gordon was not at all clever whereas I was rather unnervingly precocious so that I was soon well ahead of him in lessons and could certainly read and write passingly well by the time I was four years old. That brother Gordon in later years was to prove far more successful and alert in the matter of earning a living than I could even pretend to be is rather a poke in the eye to early developers like myself.

In anything except lessons in which Gordon appeared to be totally disinterested, there was an acute rivalry between us and, in my firmly held view, when he came out on top, it was largely due to luck which he enjoyed in far greater measure than I did. To take one example there were our Shetland ponies. When it came to giving us anything our parents were scrupulously fair. If either of us was given anything the other had to have exactly the same. Thus when Gordon was deemed old enough to have a Shetland pony I, despite my more tender years, had to have one as well.

I am not alone in my view that Shetland ponies are not really the delightful and loveable little creatures they are often cracked up to be. They are capricious and often bad-tempered to a degree. Our two ponies were, to outward appearances, identical in colour, height and sex so it was quite hard to tell them apart – at least until they were mounted. They would be reasonably docile until we got them down to the beach or on the grassy links where we could have a bit of a gallop. It was not however in their natures to have a bit of a gallop. Given the slightest encouragement and they would take off like rockets. They only knew two speeds – flat out or stop. The usual way to get them to stop was to fall off and it was here that they would show the difference in their natures.

Gordon's pony after performing a few *entrechats* and high kicks, would become perfectly docile and easy to catch again. In the case of mine, however, once it got me on the ground, no difficult matter as with my short legs it was difficult to get a grip, riding bareback, it would stop dead and proceed to try and roll on me. If I managed to foil its malevolent intentions, it would then take off and ignore all blandishments to effect its recapture until, after what seemed like hours, it decided of its own free will to give itself up.

If that should be insufficient evidence of the partiality shown to my brother by the Fates, then there was the matter of the two Shetland sheep. Again we were both given a young Shetland ewe. Unlike the Shetland ponies they were the most delightful creatures and practically in the category of household pets. The condition under which they were given was that we should be entirely responsible for seeing that they were properly fed and cared for. It was all part of a plan by Father to give us at an early age a sense of responsibility – as well perhaps as an early awareness of the facts of life. To this end it was explained to us that both our sheep were in due course to have a lamb although what other biological details were vouchsafed to us at the same time I cannot now remember.

Certainly we knew enough to know where the lambs were to come from and, in a state of high expectation, we daily examined our sheep to see if their bellies were getting any bigger. Nor was it long before there was the most indisputable evidence that Gordon's sheep was getting fatter whilst mine remained obdurately as thin as ever. Great was my chagrin when Gordon's sheep duly gave birth whilst mine remained barren.

My Aunt Carrie was up staying with us at the time and rather tactlessly asked me why Gordon's sheep had had a lamb and mine had not. To this I answered, with as much defiant pride as I could muster, 'Well, you see, my sheep is a virgin!' I cannot now remember how I came to know that there was virtue in being a virgin or, indeed, how I knew what a virgin was. The important thing about this devastating reply was that it cast a slur on the moral turpitude of Gordon's sheep and earned for me the reputation of being wise beyond my years.

Mother and Father were both very sociably minded and I have little doubt that, particularly during the long winter months, they must have found that time hung heavily on their hands. In summer the Orkney and Shetland Isles, being the part of Great Britain closest to the Arctic Circle, enjoyed almost round-the-clock daylight so that one could read a book outside at midnight. In mid-winter the sun scarcely showed itself above the skyline and the oil lamps in the house burned night and day.

Our parents' solution to boredom was to ask friends and relatives to stay. In those days the journey was an onerous one. Visitors from south of the Scottish Borders had first of all to get a train to Aberdeen and from there get a boat to Kirkwall. This, assuming that the traveller was not delayed by stormy seas, would take three days. Arriving at Kirkwall involved staying a further night or perhaps two at McKay's Hotel which was the only hotel in the town before getting one of the inter-island boats which took passengers, livestock and everything else imaginable to the out-lying islands. After a trip lasting the best part of a week, it was only polite to ask house guests to stay for a month or longer so that it was important to think carefully before sending an invitation.

It was also important for the guests to know what they were in for. To spend even a few weeks on a remote, sea-girt island without such benefits of civilization as electric light, telephone or even a wireless set and the only contact with the outside world a post, which went twice a week weather permitting, was not something to be undertaken lightly.

It was not that Father did not do his best to introduce modern technology to the island. His greatest ambition was to get a wireless set which worked. To this end, and because of the great distance from the nearest transmitting station, he caused an immensely high mast, securely anchored by guy ropes, to be erected on the front lawn.

When the work was completed, he asked all our nearest neighbours in to listen to the miraculous squeaks, grunts and whistles which came over clearly enough when the set was switched on. Most wonderful of all, occasionally very faint music could be heard and even distant voices but they were generally too far away to make out what was being said.

The novelty was not long in wearing out and, one day when the bull escaped and careered madly round the garden, it took great exception to the wireless mast and charged it, bringing it crashing to the ground. It was never put up again and the whole wireless contraption was put away for good in a cupboard.

Of all the visitors I can remember, my father's brother, Uncle Douglas, stood head and shoulders above the rest in my estimation.

Father's family consisted of five boys, of which he was the eldest. Douglas came next and, after him, Anderson and Goodwin both of whom were killed in the Great War and, finally Norland. When Grandfather died shortly after the war was over Father, as the eldest, inherited the Stronsay property and the big house in Kirkwall was sold and the proceeds divided, together with the rest of his estate, between the three surviving sons.

When Douglas and Norland came back to the islands, discharged from the army, they found themselves in the same situation as many of their contemporaries. Unqualified in any profession or trade and having to earn a living, they both emigrated to Canada. Norland set up as a stockbroker in Montreal and, some years later married a Mexican lady who, it was related, was extremely beautiful. Nobody in the family had the opportunity to judge this as, shortly afterwards, Norland disappeared and was never heard of again.

Uncle Douglas's life was altogether more exciting. Of all the five brothers who had served with distinction in the war, his record was by far the most outstanding. Whilst the four others had served in Highland regiments, Douglas, for some unknown reason, had enlisted in the Lincolns with whom he had attained the rank of Lieutenant-Colonel and a reputation for reckless bravery, verging on the foolhardy. He was awarded the DSO twice as well as the Military Cross, the Croix de Guerre and was several times mentioned in dispatches.

He went to Canada more in the spirit of adventure than with any idea of settling down to a new life. His first venture was to open a trading post on the Yukon River, near Dawson City, no doubt attracted by the already legendary tales of life on the Canadian frontier. This, apparently, did not prove to be an overwhelming success and he moved on down the Pacific coast, eventually fetching up on Vancouver Island where he got married and, immediately afterwards, joined the Canadian Mounties. Later he was to rise to a very senior post in the Mounties and, in addition, became Game Warden for British Columbia.

It must have been just before he enlisted in the Mounties that he returned to stay with us on the island. He was everything a boy could have wished for in an uncle. Nothing with Uncle Douglas was commonplace. Everything was charged with danger and adventure. I can remember him once driving my brother and me in Dad's racy open Sunbeam motor car on what passed for the road to the village which consisted of little more than a collection of fishermen's cottages around the harbour and rather grandly named Whitehall.

Naively I asked him the purpose of the little driver's mirror above the front windscreen.

'That,' said Uncle Douglas 'is a very useful piece of equipment indeed. It is so that the driver, who has to keep his eye on the road, can see if anyone in the back is going to pull a knife on him and stab him.'

This was a piece of folklore which I carried with me for many years before a more mundane explanation forced me to abandon it. In the years which followed he used to send Gordon and me the most wonderful, if impractical, presents like Canadian Mounties' hats, bowie knives and, on one occasion, two heavy plaited-leather lariats as used by cowboys for roping steers.

When the 1939–45 war broke out Uncle Douglas suddenly re-appeared and managed, despite his age, to re-enlist as a subaltern in the Seaforth Highlanders. Shortly afterwards he was posted to the 8th Army in North Africa with the rank of Colonel and later served with the British Military Mission in Greece where he was decorated with the OBE. He died of a heart attack in the airplane taking him back to England after the war was over.

For the most part, however, visitors came and went without making much impact on our daily lives, absorbed as we were in our own world of discovery. There were also moments of great excitement which stand out clearly in my memory. There was for example the time when Gordon and I were happily playing on the foreshore of St Catherine's Bay when we were suddenly alarmed to hear in the distance the outbreak of such roars and bellows as to send us hurrying in their direction to discover the cause. It turned out that Billy who worked on Dad's farm as a ploughman had been ploughing too close to a marshy little lochan just over the bank from the beach with the result that his heavy plough had tipped over into the water carrying both Billy and the horse with it. By the time we had arrived panting at the scene there was only half a horse to be seen above water whilst all that remained on view of Billy was his balding head and luxuriant moustaches, looking for all the world like an extremely angry walrus. Unable to be of much practical use in the emergency we rushed off to find help. Eventually with much heaving on ropes both Billy and his horse were dragged to safety amidst much unseemly hilarity from the rescue team.

Another great excitement was when we were allowed to go with Mum and Dad to meet the twice weekly boat from Kirkwall. No treasure galleon bearing the rich spoils of conquest can have been awaited with keener anticipation by us than the arrival of the inter-island steamer. I can remember being almost sick with excitement when the steamer was first sighted as she rounded the tip of the neighbouring island of Sanday to plough her way purposefully through the seas, the waters creaming beneath her bows or, in more stormy weather, throwing up great plumes of spray as the waves hit her when she had left the shelter of the island. When about a mile offshore, the Captain would sound three long blasts on the ship's foghorn to warn the islanders to be ready with their mail and any goods or livestock to be taken aboard.

Sometimes the excitement caused by the docking of the steamer would exceed all expectations. There was the memorable occasion when Mr Pottinger of Huip Farm was sending some of his pigs to the market. As they, with much shouting and waving of sticks, were being herded up the narrow gangway one of them made a desperate break for freedom and, with an unexpected show of athleticism, managed to leap over the handrails of the gang plank and hurl itself into the narrow space between the side of the ship and the harbour wall. Once in the water it then struck out bravely for the open sea. One of the more useless pieces of information I had gleaned by the age of four and a half now proved itself to be unexpectedly useful. It was that, should a pig for any reason go swimming, it would cut its own throat with the sharp bones of its own fore trotters. Now the opportunity presented itself to prove whether I had been correctly informed in this matter or not. The answer was that I had not.

As one of Mr Pottinger's prize porkers headed for the open sea, a dinghy was hastily launched and set off in furious pursuit. Now anyone who has not seen three men in a boat struggling to pull a large pig protestingly aboard has certainly missed a great deal. The first thing that happened was that two of the men found themselves in the water and swimming for dear life alongside the pig they had set out to rescue whilst the crowd of spectators on the quayside were beside themselves with laughter. I think that, like myself, they were all on the side of the pig. It was only after two more rowing boats had been launched that they were able to head the pig off and drive it onto the shore into the hands of a reception committee.

One of the other thrills in visiting Whitehall was when the fishing fleet put in. Stronsay, of all the Orkney Islands, had the largest fleet of herring boats so that, when they were all in the harbour, you could walk from one side of the harbour wall to the other across the decks of the tightly packed boats. Alas, today there are none.

When the boats landed their catch the herring were taken to the long shed where the fisher-wives sat, each with a crate on either side and each armed with a very sharp knife. They worked with bewildering speed, seizing a herring with one hand and, in one single motion, delivering it to the crate on the other side, cleanly gutted, with the entrails thrown into a bucket. 'Swearing like a fishwife' still remains as an expression of speech long after the fisher-women have departed. Their language was indeed ripe and quite unsuited to a boy of tender years but, despite the rigours of their work, often crouched for hours on end in a freezingly cold shed they were the most cheerful bunch of women, chattering and laughing amongst themselves and engaging in much ribald repartee at the expense of the men off the boats delivering their fish whilst their hands flew without interruption about their task.

That visits to the village, just out of comfortable walking distance for our short legs, were red letter days is not in any way to suggest that our daily lives were in any way dull. Looking back on them now they seem to sparkle with excitement and adventure.

There was one day in the week however when nothing in the world could drag us away from our own front garden. That was the day when Sandy came. Sandy drove what I suppose nowadays would be called a travelling shop but that is too mundane a description of this wonderful emporium on wheels. We could see his approach from the moment he came round the corner at Erigath about a mile distant. He sat perched high on the box of his van behind a heavy Clydesdale mare, cracking his whip while the iron-banded wheels crunched on the rutted, gritty road. There was something of the showman about Sandy. When he drew near to where we sat on either side of the garden gates, he would crack his whip all the harder shouting 'Giddyup there!' and all manner of encouragements whilst the great Clydesdale continued to clomp her way steadily forward, deaf to all the urgings of her master. She always knew from habit were and when to stop but this did not deter Sandy from shouts of 'Steady on there my beauty! Steady hup! Whoa! Whoa! Whoa!' Then, throwing the reins aside, he would leap down with the greatest agility for a man of his years and, making his way round to the back, throw open the double doors to reveal the El Dorado within.

I suppose it is the smell of things which linger longest in one's memory. Certainly the wonderful smell which hit you when Sandy opened up his 'shop' has remained with me all my life. Predominant was the smell of freshly baked bread. Sandy used a long baker's wooden shovel to retrieve the loaves of bread together with all manner of buns and cakes. In those long-ago days nothing came pre-packed. Thus there were great bins of flour or oatmeal or sugar or rice from which the required amount was weighed out and then tightly wrapped in brown paper and tied up with strong string. There was shoe polish and beeswax, mealie puddings and salted herring all mixed up with great jars of sago and rice and anything else you can imagine. Most exciting of all there was a drawer which pulled out in which was kept sweets in such profusion and of such variety that, had Gordon and I been left to decide on the rival merits of such goodies as straps of liquorice and sugar pigs, humbugs, barley sugar or chocolate cigarettes, we would be all day about it. In those days farthings, halfpence and silver threepenny pieces were common currency and many of the most desirable sweets cost a penny or less; thus the number of different items you could buy for sixpence was legion. When, after a great deal of chivying by Miss Johnstone, the selection had been finally made we were not of course allowed to gobble them all up at once. They were put in charge of Miss Johnstone and eked out each day after lunch so that they would last out exactly until Sandy came round again the following week.

Our nearest neighbours were the Stevensons who were tenants of my father and lived at the Bu Farm. The Bu, which is a name common to most of the islands, is the name by which the largest farm is known, although on an island which is largely divided into crofts, this did not necessarily amount to a great number of acres. The thing about the Bu which I found most exciting was that it was the only house I knew which had a *staircase*. Edwin, the eldest of the Stevenson children, and the one nearest to my age, told me that the only time they went 'up the stair' was to go to bed. We were never allowed to explore this mysterious region but it seemed to me to be the most wonderful way to end a day.

One of my greatest friends down at our end of the island was Peter Sinclair. Peter, as with all those of the name of Sinclair, had gipsy blood in his veins. He lived in a cottage which, from the outside, looked to be little more than a heap of stones. It was practically at the edge of the high cliffs of Rothiesholm Head and inside it was as cosy as anything you could wish for. It consisted of just one room with an oil lamp slung from the ceiling which burnt all day, come summer or winter. The only other light came from a hole in the wall on the windward side. The furniture consisted of the barest of essentials and, in one corner, there were lobster pots piled higgledy-piggledy together with all manner of other equipment for sea-fishing.

Peter himself was a small, nut-brown man dressed in a rough fisherman's jersey and a sort of tam o' shanter cap which I do not believe he ever took off. Living alone for perhaps weeks on end without seeing another soul he seemed totally content with his lot but perhaps the most remarkable thing about him of all was his knowledge of history and his gift as a story teller. It would seem unlikely that he had ever been to a school or had any formal education and there was nothing even resembling a book in his stone cabin. I suppose the stories he told must have been handed down from generation to generation. Like many of the islanders there was a timelessness about him. The only concession he would ever make to fixing a time for the events he described in such colourful detail was that they took place 'Lang afore your faither or me was born . . .'

It is not always appreciated that the Northern Isles owe nothing to the Gaelic origins of the Western Isles. The blood is mixed in with the Scandanavians. Indeed, until the islands were pledged in 1468 to James III of Scotland as part of the dowry when he married Margaret, The Maid of Norway, they had been ruled by the Norse for over five hundred years.

Peter knew the history of the islands, reaching far back into time and the names of the old Jarls, or Earls, who ruled long ago stick in my mind: he related them far more readily than the kings and queens of England and Scotland which were later to be drummed into us at school. Who could forget the names which gleam from our blood-spattered history? There was Erik Bloodaxe who was killed fighting against the English and Sigtrygg Silkybeard was, at one time, also acknowledged as King of Dublin. His successor, Earl Sigurd the Stout, was killed at the Battle of Clontarf in a desperate effort to overthrow the famed Brian Boru, the ancestor of the all-powerful O'Briens and King of all Ireland. Sigurd the Stout was succeeded as Earl of Orkney by Thorfinn Skull-Cleaver who died, rather disappointingly I could not help feeling, in his bed.

These tales of derring-do, as recounted by Peter, were all mixed up with stories of the not-so-long-ago like the days of the press gangs, for the islands were regarded as fertile ground for recruits into the British Navy, and the running fights of the smugglers and the brewers of illicit spirits against the excise men, so that all sense of chronology went out of the window. It was only many years later when I came to read the *Orkneyinga Saga*, the chronicles of the days of Norse rule, that I came to marvel at Peter's knowledge handed down, as it must have been, by story from generation to generation.

It was from Peter that we also first heard about witches. Stronsay, of all the Orkney Islands, had the reputation of being the most witch-ridden and the home of the Queen of the Witches. Her chair, fashioned out of rock, high on the cliffs at Lamb's Head from which she held Court is still there for all to see.

It is Stronsay which can also lay claim to a less enviable distinction. It was on the island that the last recorded execution of a witch took place. By what process she was tried and found guilty is not known but it was probably in the absence of any judicial authority on the island and by common complaint.

The old lady lived by Muckle Water, the only pond of any size on the island. From there she was led out to the headland at Huip about a mile away and beaten to death with corn flails. The executioners secured God's blessing for their work by first dipping their flails in holy water.

The horror of stories like these was made much worse for me by knowing exactly where they had taken place. We used to pass by Muckle Water and a ruined cottage where the witch was said to have lived, almost every day on our walks with Miss Johnstone and frequently visited Huip Farm which was owned by family friends, the Pottingers.

In our own day there was an old woman living down by the sea-shore who, it was common knowledge, was a witch. Her name was Maggie and her mother, Betty, before her was well known for her spell-weaving and feared by an earlier generation. It was generally acknowledged, in more enlightened days, that a witch would only put a hex on anyone to avenge a wrong, real or imagined done to them.

A good example of the sort of thing Maggie got up to was this. She had as a neighbour another crofter called Deedie Chalmers whom we all knew well. Between neighbouring crofters there has always been a tradition that they help one another and at times like ploughing or harvesting they pool their resources of labour and often share agricultural implements such as ploughs and so on.

It happened that this harvest had come rather later than usual so when Maggie came to ask Deedie for a hand to get her strip cut, he had not even started on his own and told Maggie that he would bring his reaper over just as soon as he got his own done. This did not suit Maggie at all. The very next day Deedie was driving his cart past the road-end of Maggie's croft when, to his great inconvenience, the axle appeared to seize up so that the cart could move neither backwards nor forwards. Of course he at once realised that this was Maggie's work but she refused to remove the spell until she got her crop cut. A story like this would become common knowledge from end to end of the island in no time at all and immediately accepted as being as true as the gospels in the Bible.

I only ever saw Maggie once although, like everyone else my brother and I knew all about her and where she lived. Whenever we went down to Rothiesholm Head we would always take the greatest care to go the long way round so as not to pass her croft. Quite why, on this occasion we had taken, against all our principles, a short cut home I cannot now, for the life of me remember. Anyway to our horror when we were almost past Maggie's cottage, we saw that she was out in front digging potatoes. Just as we thought that we could slip past without being noticed, she lifted her head and, catching sight of us, remarked in the most pleasant possible way that it was a fine afternoon. To my lasting shame we took one look at her straggling grey hair and toothless gums and ran for our lives. Nor did we stop until we were safely behind our garden wall which was over a mile away.

Looking back now on those brightly-remembered days of well over sixty years ago, what strikes me most is the *intensity* of our lives. The seasons of the year did not simply slip by with each month imperceptibly succeeding the last. Spring, the most dramatic season of all, burst upon the island with all the imperiousness of an exclamation mark. The first day of spring was not a fixed date on the calendar but, for me at any rate, the day on which the cattle were let out. Throughout all the dark days of winter they remained chained up in the byre until one morning when, with the sharp nip of spring in the air and the grass starting to show green in the fields, it was decreed that they could be freed from their winter prison. Then their neck-chains were unloosed and whoever threw open the door to freedom flattened themselves immediately against the wall so as not to be trampled underfoot in the first hectic stampede. They rushed through the doors as wild as steers at a rodeo. Matronly milk cows tossed their horns and kicked their heels like frolicsome calves in the fresh air and galloped from end to end of the field, bellowing with delight that the long dark months were over.

Perhaps it is because there are no trees in the Orkneys that spring comes so suddenly. There is none of that hesitant stop-start as the trees slowly unfold their leaves and which gives the countryside in more southerly climes that unsatisfactory in-between look with some trees in full leaf and others stubbornly bare. On the islands the ditches by the side of the roads and the dry-stone dykes which divide up the fields are almost overnight covered in flowers. Lady's smock, ragged robin and wild fuschia all seem to wake up at once to greet the first rays of a watery sun. But, most of all, spring on the islands belongs to the birds.

By the time the birds come to make their nests all the headlands are carpeted with sea pinks so that it seems almost a sacrilege to walk over them but, in the nesting season, there is a much more pressing reason for watching where you put your feet. The gulls and the terns in their colonies have their nests so close together as to make it difficult not to step on their eggs. Nor do the terns in particular make it any easier. They defend their eggs or their young chicks with an unparalleled ferocity, diving on the intruder with a totally selfless disregard for their own lives. Their razor-sharp beaks can inflict a nasty wound on an unprotected head if not worse – such as pecking out an eye.

The variety of gulls is legion, from the tiny kittiwakes to the great marauding black-backs who represented a far worse threat, to other birds' eggs or chicks, than man. In the seeming raucous disorder of these nesting colonies there is in fact a community life hedged around with the most strictly-kept rules. Whilst, in the Scottish Highlands majestic birds of prey like the golden eagle may hold sovereign rights over perhaps fifty square miles of territory, a pair of nesting gulls in a gullery are lucky if they can lay claim to five square yards which they can call their own; but this *is* their very own and let the intruder be he bird, beast or man who intrudes upon it, beware. Another thing about gulls which made great appeal to Miss Johnstone and which she explained most carefully to Gordon and me, is that they are monogamous, keeping the same mate year after year. I think perhaps that bringing this matter to our attention, was her way of preparing us for the time when we would come to learn the facts of life.

At the time I am talking about there was also a colony of puffins on our island. These mysterious birds were my favourites. During their nesting time they assume their almost absurdly bright plumage with their candy-stripe bills. Puffins nest in burrows which they dig with great energy in the sandy soil and so preoccupied are they with their tunneling and squabbling amongst themselves, that you can often pick them up when they will look at you with an air of mild surprise, tinged with reproach. As soon as you put them down again, they immediately carry on doing whatever it was that they were doing before they had been so rudely interrupted. The mysterious thing about puffins is that, the moment their chicks are ready to leave home, they shed their colourful raiment and become dull little brown birds again before disappearing out to sea, not to be seen again until the next nesting season comes round when once again they blossom out in full fig. In the Orkneys they are known as tammy-norries, which is almost as satisfying a name as kirsy-kringlos which is the islanders' name for the daddy-longlegs.

Even more spectacular are the bird colonies which nest on the high cliffs. When I was a child there was not a crack or a cranny on the weather-scarred face of the nearly vertical rocks out on the headlands which was not occupied by nesting birds. How they could survive when the stormy waves, coming in from the Atlantic, hurled themselves against the cliffs throwing the spume high in the air, would seem to be nothing short of miraculous. There were immaculately coated guillemots, each guarding a solitary sharp-pointed egg; fulmars and kittiwakes fighting for living space alongside the anti-social cormorants who, when they are marshalled together on the outlying skerries, resemble nothing more than dark-coated mourners gathered together for a wake.

There were also a number of 'everyday' birds which, all those years ago, were not in any danger of extinction but which today are numbered amongst the endangered species in Britain. For example there was the hen harrier which, when it took flight from under your feet, was an imposing bird indeed with the slow beat of its great wings and its long legs trailing behind it. Then there were the ubiquitous green plovers – peewits, lapwings, call them what you will – who were almost as intrepid as the terns in protecting their nests. I believe that the peewit was given protection in the inter-war years by the personal intervention of King George v as a result of which they became so numerous as almost to become a pest. Today, with insecticide sprays and all the other hazards to which our wild life has become heir, I believe that they are once again on the danger list.

By far the most intriguing to our young minds were the corncrakes. They made their nests in fields of growing corn. As harvesting on the islands did not take place until, if lucky, September there was no danger of the eggs being crushed by the reaper before they were hatched and, as a species, they throve mightily. At the same time they are the most shy and secretive of birds so that to catch a glimpse of one as it slipped quietly about its business was something to be remarked upon. On the other hand in the nesting season the sound of its crake was as much part of the arrival of spring as the call of the cuckoo in more southerly parts of the country. The call of the corncrake is neither a mating call nor for the purpose of advertising its presence. It is to conceal its whereabouts for corncrakes are magnificent ventriloquists. They can throw their voices to any part where they are not so as to mislead the intruder bent, as corncrakes obsessively believe, on securing the destruction of their nests. It is a brilliant and sophisticated variant of the artifice employed by more extrovert field birds of feigning a broken wing to lure predators away from their young.

Looking back now on my childhood on Stronsay, I am not sure which aspect of the crowded hours which each day brought was to play the greater part in shaping the paths in the years which lay ahead. One thing I am quite sure of is that it was an early upbringing in which neither of my parents played very much of a part.

Father was, although a very sociable man, remote from his children. I remember him as an erect, soldierly figure with a peaked hat well pulled down over his eyes after the fashion of a dragoon's helmet, forever striding off somewhere with the family Golden Labrador, Bet, at his heels in search of something to shoot or for some farm animals to herd with his walking stick. He was also, in contrast to my mother, immensely old, being somewhere in his middle thirties.

My mother was very young and of average beauty. Early photographs of her show her to have slightly protruding teeth and a glorious cascade of auburn hair. She had married at the, even for those days, extraordinarily early age of seventeen and had given birth to my brother and me by her nineteenth birthday. Again unlike father, my first memories of her were that she was always laughing. But maternal she was not.

In the same vividly-remembered way as I can now recall the bald-headed Station Master at Stirling chasing his hat down the platform, so I can recall with sharp pain one of the more intimate moments which I shared with by mother in what must have been the very early part of my life.

Mum was not a demonstratively cuddling mother anxious to show with hugs and kisses the depth of her maternal feelings for her offspring. Why she took it into her head of a sudden to try her hand at changing my nappies I cannot now imagine but that is what must have happened. In the course of inserting the large safety-pin used in those days to secure the whole thing, she somehow inadvertently managed to spear an extremely tender part of my anatomy. The screams of anger and pain with which this indignity was greeted hopefully convinced her that she was not really cut out for the more practical side of motherhood.

None of which is to say that she did not bear my brother and me great love and that this was returned in full measure.

She liked to show this by, insofar as was possible under the limitations of our island existence, surprising us with unexpected treats to which we reacted with what must have been gratifying enthusiasm.

The most sensational of all which I can remember was just before Christmas when I was four years old. It was nothing more nor less than the announcement that when our parents went on their next trip to Kirkwall we should go with them! The excitement and suspense whilst we waited for the great day when we would board the inter-island steamer and be borne off to Wonderland was almost unbearable. Nor was the realization any less glorious than the anticipation.

Kirkwall with its narrow paved streets, dominated by the magnificent cathedral of St Magnus built out of red sandstone in the twelfth century by the early Norse rulers, is one of the most picturesque of old cities imaginable but it was not its picturesqueness nor its timelessness which caused us such wonderment. The height of the buildings fronting on the harbour, some of them three storeys high, the bustle of the people on the streets and the lighted windows of the shops, glittering with Christmas decorations were things so strange to our eyes and like nothing we had ever seen before that Gordon and I were almost sick with excitement.

At that time the only hotel, or certainly hotel of any note, in Kirkwall was Mackay's which stood in all its grandeur right opposite the end of the pier where the steamers berthed. As we were gathering our bags together the gang plank was lowered but, before we had time to set foot on it, a small boy in a tight-fitting uniform and a pill box hat sprang up it, saluted smartly and, somehow gathering all the bags together darted off down again with them and set off for the hotel at a spanking pace whilst we, hand in hand with our parents, followed on in awestruck silence.

Mr and Mrs Mackay were long-standing friends of our parents so that, when we had been shown to our rooms, we all assembled in their private sitting room where the grown-ups drank grown-up drinks whilst a whole trayful of various squashes and fizzy drinks was set aside for Gordon and me from which we were urged to help ourselves. Then it was supper and bed despite our most urgent pleas that we be allowed out again. As it was we spent hours with our noses pressed to the window of our bedroom watching the comings and goings along the seafront below whilst distant lights flickered far out over the waters of Scapa Flow.

In was in the Mackays' sitting room after tea the following day that we were given the most astonishing treat of all. After a great deal of mysterious preparation when a white screen was hung on the wall and Mr Mackay spent a lot of time grunting and whistling through his teeth over a strange piece of machinery, the room was suddenly plunged into darkness. A moment later, to the accompaniment of a loud whirring noise, a beam of brilliant light illuminated the screen to be followed by jerkily animated figures acting out scenes of grippingly dramatic impact. We were watching our first Mickey Mouse cartoon. Nothing like it had ever been seen on the islands before nor, I dare say, in many places far further south.

Another highlight of this great adventure was visiting the toy shop. Whilst Gordon and I wandered through this cavern of delight, our mother (this was not a father's job) was engrossed in low-voiced conversations with the owner of the shop, the results of which were to be closely guarded secrets until Christmas morning three weeks hence – half a lifetime away. The final visit to the toy shop was on the morning of our departure. As the actually tangible results of all this to-ing and fro-ing had been disappointingly small, my brother and I, on an impulse, decided to take matters into our own hands. Whilst further whispered discussions were taking place, we filled the pockets of our coats with a great assortment of celluloid ducks, frogs and assorted fish which had been obligingly put on open display in a large tub. Although neither of us could see anything the least bit wrong in this, we still thought it prudent not to make too much noise about its at least until we had got safely back to our own cabbage patch.

In fact the whole matter did not come to light until we were undressing in front of the nursery fire at Mountpleasant prior to being given our nightly bath and when, it so happened, a grand launching of our booty was planned. That its production was not exactly greeted with the rapturous applause which we felt it rightly merited is now, with the benefit of hindsight, perhaps understandable. At the time, however, I felt that everyone had greatly over-reacted. During a pause in the lamentations and whilst father was being sent for, I took the opportunity of seizing my prizes and throwing them onto the peat fire where they went up in a most satisfactory sheet of flame.

What happened after this small show of defiance is now completely obliterated from my memory. Whatever punishment may have been meted out, it would certainly not have been condign. Perhaps the stopping of my sixpence a week pocket money but I could always get out of that one by appealing to Miss Johnstone's kindly nature. One thing is certain and that is that a fulsome letter of apology would have been sent to the owner of the toy shop and a firm lesson read to us on the subject of preserving moral standards.

That half-remembered Christmas of sixty-five years ago stays in my memory for two totally unconnected happenings. The first must seem trivial indeed. When the great ceremony of Christmas lunch was drawing to a close our mother sprang yet another of her surprises. Disappearing from the table, she appeared seconds later with an elaborately wrapped parcel bearing the name of a famous London store. After a great deal of wrestling with string and paper (it was an unbreakable rule in our house that string should never be cut but painstakingly unknotted and kept for use again on a rainy day) she triumphantly produced an elegant jar of dried figs. Fruit in general was not much seen on the island as it was hardly worth the cost and risk of bringing over something which was so readily perishable, and anything as exotic as dried figs was quite unimaginable.

I clearly remember taking my first bite of this strange wrinkled object. It tasted, to my unsophisticated palate, quite dreadful. All those nasty little seeds! I looked across the table at my brother and he too was screwing up his face quite horribly. On either side of the fireplace in the grown-ups' dining-room at Mountpleasant there were, at that time, two large glass carboys with very narrow necks. Acting as if to some unspoken command, we got down from our chairs and, marching over to the fireplace, proceeded each to stuff our half-bitten fig into the necks of the bottles. Anyone who has ever tried to recover a squashed fig from the bottom of a narrow-necked carboy will understand that this was no futile act of protest. Today, whenever I see a dried fig, the whole incident flashes before my eyes in bright technicolour. I have never tried to eat another.

The other thing by which that Christmas is remembered was of a quite different nature. We were later than usual in going to bed after that wonderful day (in spite of the figs) and sitting in our dressing gowns before the nursery fire having supper when suddenly Miss Johnstone came rushing into the room and, crossing to the window, threw back the curtains.

'Quickly! quickly! Come and look!' she cried, in a state of high excitement.

Outside the whole sky in the north was suffused with light. Then, whilst we watched, thin pencils of light swept across the heavens, growing brighter and brighter and changing through all the colours of the rainbow, then dying away only to flicker into life again before erupting into a blazing fantasy of coloured lights. At one moment the lights would fade to a will o' the wisp flicker and the next, again and again, the firmament would become ablaze as if all the bonfires of a thousand years were throwing their tongues of flame to the sky in a glorious moment of rejoicing. It was a sight the Romans had seen when they had rowed their galleons to the islands two thousand years earlier and christened them *Ultima Thule*, believing they had reached the end of the earth. It was the *Aurora Borealis*, the Northern Lights or, more picturesquely, The Merry Dancers, bringing the news of the sunlight glittering on the ice-fields of the North Pole and promising the return of Spring which was sure to come to end the long winter nights.

Spring amongst the islands brings other delights besides the nesting birds and the greening of the earth. Perhaps the most spectacular is the phenomenon of the neap tides which come with the change of the moon at the time of the spring equinox. Then, instead of the normal ebb and flow of the tide, the sea continues to ebb until it is almost out of sight so that one morning the view from our night-nursery window which looked out over St Catherine's Bay would be of nothing but a vast, and seemingly endless, expanse of sand.

The time of the neap tides is the signal for the Great Spoot Hunt to begin. 'Spoots' is the name given to the inhabitants of those long, narrow shells which are commonly to be seen washed up on shores all round Britain known as razor shells, presumably from their similarity in shape to the handle of an old-fashioned 'cut-throat' razor.

The day would scarcely have broken before figures could be seen purposefully heading for the beach bearing every sort of container from a sack to a large bucket and wielding a long knife. The spoots live just under the surface of the sand and give away their presence to the hunter by creating a small blow-hole through which they 'breathe'. The Orkney technique for catching them is not easy and requires great speed and dexterity. The method is to walk slowly backwards and, bending low with the knife poised, study the surface of the sand. As you pass over a blow-hole it will probably suddenly erupt. This means that the vibration of your footstep has caused the razor-fish to take fright and do a crash dive deeper into the sand. This sudden movement causes a jet of liquid to spout up out of the sand. Incidentally this is how they come by their odd name, spoot being simply the Orkney pronunciation of spout.

At this sign that the spoot is about to make its escape, the hunter must immediately plunge the knife into the sand and, with a quick circular motion, bring the mollusc to the surface. Surprisingly they are very fast movers indeed. The expert will know exactly which way it is moving and thus know where to plunge the knife so that his bucket will be quickly filled whilst that of the less skilful will remain obdurately empty. A top spoot-catcher will average about one success in two stabs whereas the amateur will be lucky to connect once in ten.

I do not know whether anyone bothers to go spoot catching nowadays but there are many other methods which used to be used in different parts of the country. By far the most simple is to pour a little table salt into the blow-hole whereupon the spoot will shoot to the surface of its own accord, rather than endure the increased salinity. On the islands in those days table salt was far too valuable a commodity to be wasted on catching spoots.

Spoots are considered a great culinary delicacy by those in the know. A by-product of the Great Spoot Hunt in the Spring following the Christmas-of-the-Dried-Figs was when Mother once again decided to spring one of her surprises. This time it was nothing less than that she would *herself* cook a dish of spoots which she had acquired from one of the expert spoot-hunters. It was, she decided, far too delicate a task to be entrusted to our beloved cook, Harriet Hourston, although mother's claims to *Cordon Bleu* status in the kitchen were not the stuff of which legends are made.

Well-wishers had warned Mum that spoots, when cooked, tended to be on the tough side. It was something which, she decided, could be got round easily enough by boiling them for a long time. So she set about the task and soon the whole house became permeated with the smell of boiling spoots. Every couple of hours or so Mum would go through to the kitchen and give them a tentative prod with a fork. And so it went on, hour after hour. The whole operation had started soon after breakfast. At nightfall she decided that the solution might be to leave them to simmer on a low heat over night. By midday the following morning there was really nothing for it but to take them off the stove and serve them up for lunch with an elaborate white sauce. They were of the consistency of thick leather boot-laces and tasted, so far as one was able to judge, of the insides of golf balls.

The correct way to cook this delicacy, as Harriet would have been only too glad to tell her, is to drop them in their shells into scalding water just long enough for the shells to open and then cook the flesh very lightly in milk. They are then said to become as tender as young chickens and to have just as delicate a flavour.

It was the sea which perhaps, of all the influences of my early childhood, was the most dominant. It could hardly have been otherwise, living as we did on a relatively small speck of land in the middle of great oceans. There was not a family on Stronsay which did not scrape at least some part of its living from the sea. Apart from the herring fishing fleet of seine netters whose main harbour amongst the Orkneys was Whitehall, everyone up and down the island had their own small rowing boat and a few lobster pots which they worked off their own bit of the shore or from which they would spend a summer's evening handlining for any of the great variety of fish in the richly-endowed waters.

Of all the fish which it was the greatest fun for us to try our skill at catching, the mackerel was the favourite – largely because, if one got the time and place right, it required no skill at all! When there was a shoal of mackerel close enough inshore their presence was easy enough to spot from the excited activity of flocks of gulls or other sea birds diving into the water for an easy meal. The birds were not feeding off the mackerel but the sand eels on which the mackerel also like to feed and whose attack upon them had forced them to near the surface. Thus, torpedoed from below by the mackerel and dive-bombed from above by the sea birds, the lot of the sand eels was not a happy one.

All the equipment that was required to catch the mackerel was a weighted handline to which was attached a number of hooks, dressed only with a wisp of feather. You let this down over the side of the boat and, at the sign of a tug, pulled it in again as rapidly as possible. The fisherman would be unlucky not to find almost every hook occupied. So voracious were the mackerel when feeding that even the formality of a feather was scarcely necessary to attract them. Quite often they would attach themselves to a bare hook.

Another fish with suicidal tendencies is the kuithe which is the islanders' name for the coal fish when it is a year old and weighing something between a half and three quarters of a pound. They can be caught easily from the rocks simply by clambering onto a rock armed with a short stick and a line tied to the end with two or three feathered hooks. No fancy fly-casting is required. Plunge the whole rod into the deep water and swish it with a rapid scything action. On being brought out of the water it will be found, in almost every case, that your breakfast has become attached to the hooks.

Although fishing for the crofter was for the most practical of reasons, i.e. to feed his family, the catching of lobsters was, even in those days, a much more commercial proposition. They could be taken into the dealers in Whitehall and exchanged for real money to be sent south to grace the tables of the rich. For a family to eat their own lobsters would have been regarded as the height of extravagance if not downright eccentricity.

In those far-off days it was not at all unusual to see schools of whales plunging out in the bay or dolphins frolicking off the rocks. The commonest of the whales were what were known as the 'caa'ing whales' from the Scottish word to 'caa' which means to drive. These are the bottle-nose whales which are today, in common with most species of whale, becoming increasingly rare. Another name for them is the pilot whale because of their habit, which amounts to a compulsion, of following their appointed leader, the pilot, right onto the shore. There have been many instances where the leader, becoming for some undiscovered reason disorientated, has led a great school of whales onto a beach and where all efforts to tow these huge monsters off and re-direct them again seawards has proved unsuccessful.

In earlier times the islanders, if a school of caa'ing whales was spotted close enough to the shore, would set out in small boats and with a great deal of shouting and banging of drums, seek to drive them onto the beach to be slaughtered. Of all the beaches amongst the islands our beach at Rothiesholm was considered to be the finest of all the killing grounds. Those days are now happily long past but on the Faroe Islands the whale hunt, or *Grindabod* as it is known, is still carried out and a successful one still a cause for great feasting and celebration amongst the Faroese.

All in all the sea is regarded by the islanders as a cruel mistress but a bountiful one. In the past even shipwrecks were regarded as a heaven-sent bounty and a gift from the deep. In the last century there was a minister on our immediately neighbouring island of Sanday whose Sunday prayer was alleged to end: 'If it be Thy will that ships should run upon the rocks, we pray Thee Lord in Thy Goodness not to forget Thy humble servants on Sanday.' It was always about another island that stories like this were told!

Although for me each day brought with it its own immediate excitements so that I could not conceive what it was like to be bored, there was also a timelessness about life. The past crowded in very closely on the present so that long ago became yesterday and fact was often overtaken by fiction.

All of the Orkney Islands bear a tangible testimony to the mysterious tribes who inhabited them two thousand years ago when Rome was the capital of the civilised world and long before the Norwegian long boats emerged from the mists to conquer the islands with fire and sword. It was the age of the broch builders. The brochs, whose ruined remains are to be found on headlands all over Orkney and Shetland as well as the north of Scotland, were strongly fortified houses whose exact purpose has never been satisfactorily explained. To repel invaders perhaps – but what invaders? Or as primitive castles from which the leading families ruled their fellow tribesmen?

Out on Lamb Head on Stronsay there are the remains of a broch which it is still possible to climb into and crawl along lengths of flagged passageways where they have not been blocked by falls of stone, centuries earlier. It was a regular playground for Gordon and me and of no more historical significence in our young lives than a ruined croft by the seashore. Like most broch remains, it has never been excavated but on Mainland there are sites like the well-known Scara Brae which attracts thousands of visitors a year. Amusingly the stone flags of Scara Brae carry the graffiti scribblings of much earlier visitors, the Norse, being, amongst other ruderies, such inscriptions as the Norse equivalent of the last war, 'Killroy was here' variety. On the broch out on Lamb Head, Gordon and I left our own scribblings which, perhaps fortunately, may not have withstood the same test of time.

> Who can see the Green Earth any more
> As she was by the sources of time?
> Who imagines the fields as they lay
> In the sunshine unworn by the plough?
> Who think as they thought,
> The tribes who them roamed on her breast
> Her vigorous sons?

These are questions posed by Matthew Arnold in his poem 'The Future'.

There must be many corners of the Green Earth where a couple of thousand years 'are but a moment gone' and our childhood playground on Stronsay certainly cannot be far off being one of them.

Even the folklore of the island had its own immediacy. I do not think that I ever believed in Father Christmas or that I thought of charming stories like The Babes in the Wood or Snow White and the Seven Dwarfs to be other than delightful flights of imagination but the folk tales of the island were quite a different matter. They were very much for real.

The belief in a race of mischievious little men – the forerunners of the Royal Air Force Gremlins of the last war – is common to most island folk. On Stronsay they were known as the 'hillie-trows' and the mischief they could get up to limitless. It could be quite a small matter like turning the milk sour or more important misdemeanours such as taking an unguarded baby from its cot and leaving a changeling in its place.

The hillie-trows lived underground and their places of residence were well known. Few would dare to pass them after sundown. There were certain nights when they came out to dance and anyone passing one of their mounds when they did so and who heard their music would find it so irresistible that they could not refrain from joining in. It was related that one farmer, returning from an evening of celebration, rashly passed by. Immediately entranced, he leapt into the circle of dancers and footed it with the best of them. It was only when he got home that he found that the harvest had come and gone and that his dancing had lasted six months.

There were also the folk who lived under the sea and were known as 'Selkies'. They, too, sometimes came ashore to dance, shedding their seal skins which they habitually wore in their underwater world. One of the stories told to us round the fireside was of another farmer who saw the Selkie-folk dancing and, creeping down to the shore, stole one of the seal skins. Thus when the time came for the Selkies to return to the sea, there was one of them, a truly lovely maiden, left without the means of escape. Fortunately she fell in love with the farmer, married him and bore him several children. They were as happy as the day was long and she only grew restless on those nights when the Selkies came ashore to dance. On one such night when her husband was out, she came across her old seal skin abandoned in a cupboard. When her husband returned she had gone, reclaimed by her own folk. It was said that she returned from time to time to visit her children but her sorrowing husband never saw her again.

There were others like the 'Fin-men' who were married to mermaids and could perform fantastic feats of oarsmanship in the dangerous roost tides which at certain seasons raced through the islands, bringing destruction to many a craft caught unawares. People like the Fin-men were just as real to us as the Dan Dares of modern schoolboy fiction and their feats of derring-do every bit as impressive. It was said of the Fin-men that it only took them seven strokes of the oar to cross the North Sea from Orkney to Norway.

One of the islands traditionally inhabited by the Fin-men was Eynhallow which lies in close to Mainland and which is frequently cut off by the most terrifying rip-tides. In legend Eynhallow was also said to be one of the vanishing islands which had a habit of appearing and disappearing into the mists, which is, in fact, what the real islands are apt to do.

There was a distinguished Moderator of the Church of Scotland whose house looked out over the water to Eynhallow. He was once asked teasingly by a friend if he really believed that the island could disappear at any time. 'I never go upstairs without pausing on the landing and peeping through the window to see if it is still there' he replied in all solemnity.

This running together of past and present and intermingling of reality and fable are the strands from which the cloth is woven and is something which is common to all island children. It is a heritage which stays with us all, by and large, for the rest of our lives.

The first inkling that for me the dream was about to end came when, completely out of the blue, Mother announced that she was going to make a journey down to Scotland. Such a thing was, in my young life, unheard of. Certainly we had not lacked for visitors to Mountpleasant from faraway places but they might have been from outer space, so little did my brother and I relate to them. We had been brought up in a world without newspapers, telephones or radio and the picture books from which we had learned to read depicted a world which seemed dangerous indeed. Trees, for example, were outside our experience and were imagined as places where wild animals stalked and great serpents crouched in their branches, poised to strike with deadly effect at the unwary passer-by. When we went to see Mother off on the boat, there was a heavy dread in our hearts that we would never see her again.

For weeks there was an uneasiness in the air and then, with the same suddenness as Mother's departure had been announced, the next blow fell. She was not coming back to the island but we were to join her at our grandmother's house in distant Perthshire, half way down on the map, to England.

I do not remember that there were tears or expostulations at this news. Rather a deep-inside feeling of excitement rather in the way one was to feel later in life just before the kick-off of an important football game.

Hot on the heels of this development there came more stupendous news. Miss Johnstone was going to get married! We had been vaguely aware that she had a gentleman friend who was a hairdresser in Kirkwall and, appropriately, called Mr Shearer. The plan was that Miss Johnstone was to take us over to Kirkwall where she was to deliver herself into the arms of Mr Shearer after handing us over to the care of Mr and Mrs Mackay of the hotel who were to arrange for our onward transmission under escort to Perthshire.

I clearly remember a problem which cropped up immediately before our departure. Gordon and I had somehow come into possession of a small rose bush which was quite an acquisition on the island. There was much agonising about where it should be planted which was made much more immediate because of our imminent departure. It was already late summer and with winter round the corner it would have to be in a sheltered spot to protect it from the coming gales. It was only on the morning when we were about to leave to catch the boat that a decision was finally reached. Amidst violent protests from Miss Johnstone that we would get our hands, which we had just washed, dirty again, the job was accomplished. For good measure, with Dad honking the car horn impatiently, we fenced it in with some old tin sheets.

My last recollection is of leaning over the rails of the steamer looking down at Dad in his plus-fours and his cap pulled down over his eyes, looking very sad and dejected as he waved us goodbye.

Then, for the first time, I wept.

CHAPTER THREE

Shades of the prison-house begin to close
Upon the growing boy,
But he beholds the light, and whence it flows,
He sees it in his joy;
The youth, who daily travels farther from the east
Must travel, still is Nature's priest,
And by vision splendid,
On his way attended.
Intimations of Immortality William Wordsworth.

Our grandmother's house, Wester Kinloch, stood on a gently sloping hillside looking out over a wide and lush valley, the heartland of some of Scotland's richest agricultural acres and the centre of the fruit growing industry. The contrast with the bleakness of our beloved Orkney could not have been more absolute.

The house itself was, to put it modestly, imposing and, to our childish eyes, with its high panelled entrance hall and broad sweep of staircase leading up to the portrait gallery from which ancestors gazed down arrogantly on the intruder, just a little scary.

If the house was imposing, Grandmother was even more so. My recollection is that it was only after we had been installed in our nursery quarters for several days that we were taken to meet her. The audience was given at teatime and took place in a room known as the Chinese Boudoir. It was customary in those days for ladies of quality to entertain other ladies of quality in their boudoirs which constituted a kind of private sitting-room. It was then also the height of fashion for boudoirs to be tricked out in Chinese fashion with intricately woven screens and all manner of other *chinoiserie* and furnished with Chippendale's furniture of his Chinese period. The boudoir was essentially a ladies-only room and for any lady to invite a man on his own into her boudoir was the height of impropriety.

The effect of meeting our grandmother for the first time in these surroundings was awesome. She sat, regally upright, on a high-backed embroidered-tapestry chair behind an impressive spread of silver tea things, arrayed on a Chinese lacquer table. Our mother who was, as it were, presenting us at Court, sat between us looking rather harrassed and twisting a small lace handkerchief in her anxious hands. If my description of the scene is not correct in every detail, the impression it left on my young mind is not in anyway at fault. I remember too that we were given very thinly-cut sandwiches and brandy-snaps filled with freshly whipped cream which I have continued to regard ever since as one of the greatest of all teatime treats.

Granny now became, if largely by remote control, the single most important person in our lives. Our paths only crossed occasionally but not a sparrow could fall without Granny getting to know of it instantly. She was in very truth the mistress of all she surveyed and there was not a servant in the house nor an employee on the estate who did not go in awe of her.

All our meals were taken in the nursery but our presence was required once a week, for luncheon (always luncheon – never 'lunch') on Sunday in the dining room. Sometimes there were other guests but whether there were or if it was just us, the meal always developed into a running instruction on decorum, etiquette and table manners. Her eagle eyes from the end of the table never missed a trick.

'Douglas!' she would exclaim, breaking off whatever she was saying, 'How often have I told you always to tip your plate away from you when you are finishing your soup?'

'Why, Granny?' I might ask, greatly daring.

'Because Granny does not wish to see the bottom of your plate.' End of message.

The pudding course always had to be eaten employing both a spoon and a fork – even if it was ice cream. 'Never talk with your mouth full' she would suddenly remark, regardless of the fact that neither my brother nor I hardly ever uttered a word, in obedience to the precept that 'children should be seen and not heard'. Children could only take their chairs after all the adults were seated and must always sit bolt upright without touching the back of the chair. 'Stop *lounging*!' Granny would snap if one, for the merest moment, neglected to observe this rule.

Oddly enough I do not remember particularly resenting this regime but it was always with a sense of great relief when, before coffee was served to the grown-ups, we were allowed to 'get down'. (Remembering never to run until we got outside the dining-room door.)

Granny's whole life was devoted to keeping up her social position to the exclusion of practically everything else. This took the form of establishing, for the benefit of anyone who cared, that she represented 'old money' with family roots which were both ancient and aristocratic. There can never have been a time when it was more important for socially ambitious families, the origin of whose wealth lay in the Industrial Revolution of the nineteenth century, to try to distance themselves from being regarded as *nouveau riche* and establishing themselves as being part of the old social order. Perthshire was, and to a lesser degree still is, the most sensitive of all Scottish counties when it comes to trying to establish the distinction between 'County' and 'Trade'.

By and large this phenomenon springs from the establishment of the jute trade, of which Dundee had a near monopoly, early in the nineteenth century. It was not long before Dundee was rivalling some of the great industrial centres in the Midlands of England and family dynasties with their fortunes founded in the trade were springing up like the hosts of Midian each vying with the next one to build higher and higher smoke-belching chimney stacks.

It soon became fashionable for the newly rich industrialists to establish family seats for themselves in the country and Perthshire with its grouse moors and salmon-rich rivers provided the perfect gentlemanly environment. Not an estate came on the market but it was eagerly snapped up. One of the most powerful and prolific of the jute families were the Coxes. In the second half of the nineteenth century they acquired between them so many large houses and estates that Perthshire became known to the irreverent as Cox-shire.

That my grandfather should have acquired his considerable wealth from the family Works during this period was something that Granny was prepared to go to almost any lengths to conceal.

In fact the family business was founded in 1828 by Grandfather's great-uncle, one of a family of eight brothers and sisters. It was only due to the most fortunate circumstance that none of them produced a male heir save Grandfather's father, who predeceased him, so that he inherited the business. In Granny's eyes there were only two slightly mitigating circumstances. The first was that The Chapel Works were not in Dundee but in Montrose and the second that its business was not in jute but in flax.

'Your grandfather was *not* in jute but in flax which is *quite a different thing*', as she never tired of reminding us. The inference being that to be a flax merchant was to be quite a few points higher up the social scale than a jute tradesman. When Grandfather died in 1910 she moved with lightning speed to dispose of all the family shares to a distant cousin and thus finally washed her hands of the whole unfortunate business.

She had married Grandfather as her second husband quite late in his life and he seems to have indulged her social aspirations by having a great number of family trees researched including one of Granny's which strove, without a great deal of conviction, to show that she herself had landowning connections. In fact his own antecedents were far more impressive, as the family portraits which hung in such profusion round the gallery testified.

Grandfather, James Middleton Paton, was descended through the female line from the Earls of Middleton. The first Earl of Middleton fought valiantly on the side of Oliver Cromwell and commanded the Parliamentarian Army in Scotland against the great Royalist General the Marquess of Montrose on whom he inflicted a rare defeat at the battle of Aylth. He then changed sides and, espousing the cause of Charles the Second, joined him in exile in Cologne.

He must have been a colourful character. Heavily in debt, the Sheriff's Officer attempted to serve a notice on him, sequestering his estates. He had the man boiled and served as soup to his tenants. This incident may have hastened his departure to the other side of the Channel. He married his second daughter, Lady Helen, to the Ist Earl of Strathmore of Glamis Castle, the ancestor of our present Queen who settled all his debts for him *in absentia*. I have always thought this chivalrous act to have been a dreadful waste of money. Even now I sometimes catch members of the Queen's family, the Bowes-Lyons, eyeing me speculatively, perhaps weighing up the chances of ever getting this money repaid. No chance now I fear.

He was created an Earl by Charles II after the restoration and was further rewarded by being installed as the Lord High Commissioner for Scotland. He did not hold this high office for very long nor, by all accounts, did he ever draw a sober breath. He was shuffled off to be Governor of Tangier instead, an office he held for ten years before breaking his neck falling downstairs drunk.

The second Earl was a very different kettle of fish. Brought up at the Court of Charles II, he had a distinguished ambassadorial and Parliamentary career and had the difficult task of managing the House of Commons for James II before joining him in exile in France where he acted as his Secretary of State, as he did for his successor James Edward, 'The Old Pretender'. He died in exile at St Germain. The title has been in abeyance ever since.

All of which was a great source of satisfaction to Granny, particularly the family connection with Glamis. When Elizabeth Bowes-Lyon, the present Queen Mother married the then Duke of York, later George VI, she took to counting how many removes in cousinship there were and then, mentally, halfing them.

Of more immediate interest to my brother and I, as a result of the sudden change in our life-style as it was lived at Wester

Kinloch, were the household and outdoor staff whose number was legion and with whom we were in daily contact. Oddly, I cannot now remember who first filled the role of governess – nanny charged with the running of our day-to-day existence but undoubtedly the most important person and the one who commanded our greatest affection was Lizzie. I suppose her title would have been head-housemaid. She operated from her own headquarters which was styled Lizzie's Pantry and which for us was a haven of delight and often of refuge.

The supreme ruler of the domestic scene was the head cook who ruled from the stove of her great cavernous kitchen which was, for us, strictly forbidden territory. She was called Mrs Frost and was only occasionally to be glimpsed moving like a majestic sailing ship with an escort of twittering kitchen and scullery maids following in her wake. She was, by all accounts, a wonderful cook but, as is not uncommon in the world of fine cookery, temperamental to a degree. Gardening boys bringing the daily selection of fruit and vegetables to the kitchen door, quailed before her as she inspected their offerings and even Granny watched her step when planning the day's menus lest, by a careless word, she might offend and bring on a tantrum.

Lizzie was everything that Mrs Frost was not. She was a tiny little person, neat as a new pin in her sparkling white apron and cap, with a sort of screwed-up face like a walnut. She was a survival from Grandfather's day and had been 'promoted', on the birth of my mother, from being a young parlourmaid to being assistant to her nanny. In the complicated hegemony of a Victorian household to be nursery staff as opposed to run-of-the-mill house domestic brought with it all manner of small advantages and even privileges. For Lizzie it signalled the point from which her whole life became dedicated to the family with whom she had first gone into service as a fourteen-year-old orphan from Wick, one of the most northerly and remote townships in Scotland.

Lizzie's pantry was a narrow, dark room with a small barred window at the far end and above a sink where all the washing up of the more delicate china and glass was done as her sole responsibility. It was lined from floor to ceiling on both sides with cupboards which had sliding doors which concealed all manner of delightful and intriguing things. By no means least was the one nearest to the door where cakes, biscuits and other goodies were kept in a great variety of tins and a glass jar of bullseyes which I strongly suspect were bought out of Lizzie's own money.

It was in this room that Lizzie had her whole being from the time she came down to prepare the morning tea trays until she went up the servants' staircase to bed, having washed up the dinner glasses. She had only one extravagance which was a twopenny woman's magazine which was very popular at the time, called the *Red Letter*, and which was crammed with romantic love stories and which she read avidly from cover to cover. She never ever went out. Once Granny attempted to encourage her by buying her a gleaming new Raleigh bicycle. This she kept in a cupboard off the servants' hall and took it out once a week to give it a thorough polishing but I do not think she ever learned to ride it.

Lizzie stayed with the family all her days, only returning to live with her two spinster sisters in Wick a few months before her death when she was well over eighty. Nobody took more interest or pride in the activities and achievements of anyone who was 'family'. She was for us, from the very beginning in those far off days, a rock to which we clung.

Of the outdoor staff there were two people who were of outstanding importance in our lives. The first was Granny's chauffeur, Mr Page. It was a strict rule, incidentally, that all senior staff as well, of course, as tenants should be addressed by us, as children, by their correct title unlike the usual practice by grown-ups of using their surnames only. Mrs Frost, as cook, was always given the courtesy title of Mrs, even by Granny herself, although she was unmarried but, in our world, Page the chauffeur became Mr Page and Clarke, and the head gardener Mr Clarke. Only their children or junior staff could be addressed by their first names as they would address us.

Mr Page's territory was the large six-car garage behind the stable block as well as the engine room which housed the engine which provided power for the electric light and which was also his responsibility. Mr Page had one great ability which totally amazed us. He could stand on his head! He would do this to entertain us at any time of the day and we never tired of asking him. Whilst carrying out this feat he never took off his flat chauffeur's hat and as his chauffeur's uniform also consisted of blue serge riding breeches and high leather boots the spectacle was indeed an entrancing one.

Granny had, at that time, a large Daimler motor-car with a glass partition which separated the driver from the passengers. When she wished to communicate with Mr Page, which was frequently, she would blow vigorously into a speaking tube which produced a whistle by the driver's ear. He would then remove a plug from his end of the apparatus and thus communication was established. Driving with Granny was altogether an exciting business and attended with great ceremony. Granny took her place on the nearside of the back seat. Whatever the weather and no matter how short the journey might be, she always had herself tucked in under a large lion-skin fur rug and a basket was provided containing thinly cut sandwiches and flasks of tea and coffee lest there should be an outbreak of hunger or thirst on the journey. Thus ensconced she would be driven very slowly to Blairgowrie or, less frequently, Perth, raising her hand in gracious greeting to whoever was passed, whether she happened to know them or not, rather after the manner of Queen Mary.

Mr Clarke, the head gardener, was a man who, even in his work clothes looked, with his well-trimmed beard and side-whiskers, the epitome of a Victorian English gentleman down to the last button of his waistcoat and heavy silver watchchain. However his eyes twinkled and he dearly loved a joke. On our frequent visits to the big walled garden set up above the house with the most splendid views over the countryside, he would always break off whatever he was doing, which was usually supervising the work of the gardener's boys in some activity, to greet us with the greatest of old-fashioned courtesy. As often as not, he would then lead us up to the greenhouses which ran across the whole of the north wall, to select peaches or grapes or anything else in season which he would present to us with great ceremony. He also took all the time in the world to show us some new, exotic bud about to come into flower or explain what he was planting to come into bloom in the following year. After the bareness of our garden plots on Stronsay such almost tropical luxuriousness was quite stupefying.

The sudden migration from Stronsay had taken place in the late summer when all the Perthshire countryside had been in full fig. The first crowded weeks were so totally bewildering that only the impressions remain stamped in my mind. There is no memory of any routine being established as I had known it. There are no recollections of daily walks or afternoon lessons in reading and writing which we had had with Miss Johnstone nor do I recall or if we had daily baths or if Mum came up to tuck us into bed each night.

It was only with the coming of autumn, and the (to us) novel spectacle of falling leaves whilst the whole countryside turned from green to brown, that some sort of pattern became established. Most of our time was spent out-of-doors with at least one 'organised' walk a day. The house looked out over a large expanse of water, Marlee Loch, and the novelty of what seemed to us to be a small placid inland sea, untroubled by storms or tides fascinated us. There was a large boathouse by the lochside which was always kept locked and even the two rowing boats inside kept securely chained. Dreadful warnings were given of the dangers of our venturing out on the loch without an adult in charge. Accustomed as we were to life on Stronsay where nothing was ever kept locked, not even the house doors, we thought this rather droll; however it did have the effect of making the prospect of an outing on the water something to be looked forward to with the greatest excitement.

These days on the loch were the subject of the most meticulous planning. In the first place it required the services of Mr Page which meant in turn that a day had to be selected when Granny did not want to go out in her car. Then an exact time had to be settled for the start of the expedition and a time by which we had to return. If, treat of all treats, it was decided that we should take a picnic the whole administrative problem became doubly complicated whilst we fretted with impatience.

When it was finally mounted, the entire operation was put into the hands of Mr Page who was in sole charge and directly responsible for our safe return. We must have looked a strange sight as we set off, skipping with delight down the rhododendron-lined drive, with Mr Page marching along stiffly behind in his full chauffeur's uniform including his peaked hat. The moment we were out of sight of the house however Mr Page became a changed man. It became immediately apparent that he was looking forward to the outing just a much as we were. He loosened the top buttons of his uniform, pulled off his tie and, if he did not exactly skip, his step lightened and his whole being took on the jaunty air of someone just let out of school.

Marlee Loch has always been noted for the immense variety of its bird life. There was every species of waterfowl imaginable; coots and waterhens swam jerkily in and out of the reed beds; herons stood silently sentinel on the shore and wild swans sailed majestically by whilst every species of duck rose in protesting flocks as we rowed past. There was a small island on the loch where we could land. Led by Mr Page who was by now perspiring heavily as a result of his efforts on the oars, we would push our way through the undergrowth to come on the nesting sites of a hundred birds awaiting their owners' return in the Spring.

There were even greater excitements on those first voyages of discovery. Once, when we were rowing close to a large bed of water lilies, there was a sudden swirl in the water and a splash as something did a crash dive into the depths.

'A pike!' exclaimed Mr Page. 'An' by God, thon was a big 'un!'

Naturally we were agog with excitement and Mr Page was quite up to the occasion. As we rowed on he waxed lyrical on the subject of pike. Marlee, it appeared, unlike most Scottish lochs, was not a trout fisherman's paradise but given over almost entirely to pike and perch. Indeed the pike were famous throughout the country for their size and ferocity. Great and wonderful were the stories we heard.

As we came round a spur of land, Mr Page rested on his oars and allowed the boat to glide on. 'We are just about to pass over the deepest water of the whole loch' he told us. 'It was here that the farmer, old Jock Menzies that would be, was loading a cart with turnips in that field over there. It was in the middle of a heavy cold spell with the loch half frozen over. Something caused the horse pulling the cart to take fright and it bolted, pulling the load of turnips behind it, right out onto the ice. It was about thirty yards out before it broke through the ice and disappeared. Neither horse nor cart were ever seen again. *That's* how deep it is hereabouts!'

We gasped in wonderment, but he held up his hand for silence. 'There is something else I am telling you which I saw with my own eyes. I was standing ower by thon tree watching a goose out here on the water. A muckle great goose it was too. Suddenly it gave a kind of squawk and started to flap its wings but it couldna get into the air. Something had grabbed it and was pulling it under. It was a monster pike. Down there,' he said as we all gazed over the side of the boat, 'there are pike bigger than you would ever believe. Some say they weigh a hundred pounds or more.'

There was the story too which we then heard of Marlee's own Loch Ness monster. There was someone out fishing in the hotel boat when, right up at the top end of the loch, he got hooked into a big pike. At first he thought that he had hooked a log on the bottom but as he tugged the 'log' started to move and set off steadily down the loch towing the boat behind it. Having got rather over half a mile down the water, the fish took it into its head to dive into the reed beds and, with an impatient shrug, snapped the thick wire trace like a piece of cotton. Since then there have been repeated reports of a similar encounter with an apparently massive fish.

'He's still out there somewhere' said Mr Page, gazing out

over the water and looking suddenly like the latter day dedicated shark hunter in *Jaws*.

Marlee Loch had another magic for us. As dawn broke one morning I was awakened by a sound the like of which I had never heard before. It was like the rush of wind in the tree tops with a wild chorus of cries tossed about in a gale. The geese had arrived.

The arrival of the wild geese, migrating down from the barren wastes of the Arctic, was an annual event which could be accurately anticipated to within a few days. They were pink feet and greylag with the very occasional Canadian visitor and they came in their thousands. Looking out of the window the whole surface of the loch seemed to be grey with them and still they were arriving in battalions, planing in on stiff wings until they were over the water and then plunging in a spectacular corkscrew dive to join their companions whilst the clamour of exchanged greetings rose to a crescendo.

The coming of the geese was not an event that was greeted with universal joy. The farmers, on the higher ground, in particular, regarded them as the complete opposite of a blessing. Once in residence they would set off at first light for their feeding grounds on the upland stubbles and potato fields. A large flock of geese on a potato field could, if undisturbed for a few hours, wreak total havoc. They would stay on the loch until, in the early Spring, of one accord they would start the long journey back to their northerly nesting grounds. Within hours they would all be gone.

Geese were not the only wildlife which reached plague proportions. The rabbits were even worse. To go out first thing in the morning and clap your hands was to see the whole of the parkland in front of the house start into life as the hordes of rabbits made a concerted rush to the rhododendron bushes where they had their burrows. From time to time a major offensive would be launched against the rabbits. The most effective weapon was the long net which was commonly used by poachers in their night operations. A long net is approximately forty yards long with a running cord on its bottom edge. On a really big rabbiting night half a dozen of these might be used, end to end, so as to cover the whole of one side of a field. The way the nets were operated was this:

Each net was hung on a series of thin, notched willow sticks. The method of fixing the nets had to be very carefully observed, using a running hitch. A wrongly tied knot could ruin the whole operation if, when a rabbit hit the net, it did not run smoothly. Setting the nets was breathlessly exciting work. It had to be done in total darkness and soundlessly. They were set as close as possible to the field fence so as to cut off the rabbits, who would be out in the field feeding, from their burrows. One careless stumble in the dark and they would be alerted and make a dash for home prematurely. This accomplished, the netting party would make its way silently by a circuitous route to the other side of the field and the drive would start. Torch lights would be switched on and the more noise the better. With the net 'running' properly, when a rabbit hit it it would become enmeshed in it rather like a bag and the more the victim struggled, the more inextricably it became enmeshed.

I am rather surprised now that Gordon and I were allowed to go out on these night expeditions. Perhaps Granny was not informed but go we did and it was a proud honour for me when I was trusted to tie the slip knots. I really believe now that, sixty-five years later, I could still do it!

If I have up to this point shown Granny as a tiresome, tyrannical and snobbish old lady with too much money, it is not in fact to give an entirely fair picture. There were other aspects to her character which I was only able to appreciate in later years. Far from being puritanical, she was fond of her drink and smoked like a chimney but she had another weakness which I was to find particularly endearing. She gambled ferociously. Not, fortunately, for large sums of money or to an extent which has beggared many much wealthier families, but with obsessive dedication. Not a day passed but the daily papers were closely studied and her selections made. Her great weakness was for two shilling accumulators and a peculiarly complicated bet which she was to explain to me in detail many years afterwards, known as a Yankee. The result of these deliberations was then committed to paper and sent in to the Blairgowrie bookmaker via one of the gardener's boys on a bicycle. The whole operation was supposed to be shrouded in the deepest secrecy. She hid behind a *nom de plume* and, to the end of her days, she believed that her cover had never been blown. Her *nom de plume* was Frou-Frou.

As Christmas approached we had a great surprise. One day when we were setting out for our morning walk we were met in the hall by a large, bluff man who shook Gordon and me gravely by the hand and announced that he was our Uncle John.

Uncle John, it turned out, was our mother's younger brother and had just returned for the Christmas vacation from Cambridge where he was reading history at Trinity College. All of this meant nothing to us but we accepted that this big friendly man was our uncle gladly enough and, later on, with enthusiasm. I think now, looking back, that Uncle John was a very shy man, perhaps even introverted, and he overcame this by always speaking in a very loud voice, exuding bonhomie, and generally stamping around the place like a bull elephant. He was the first grown-up who actually played games with us, enlisting whoever was around to join in games such as Last Across, Pig-in-the-Middle and Tag. His likeness to a bull elephant was made the more real for us by his habit of trumpeting loudly and frequently, blowing his nose into an enormous white handkerchief.

One morning Uncle John announced that he was going off to have 'a shot at the duck'. It was not long before he returned and produced out of his game-bag for all of us to admire, two plump domestic Aylesbury ducks. It appeared that he had simply strolled down to the Home Farm and let off both barrels at the Aylesburys, swimming around innocently on the duck-pond! Accustomed as we were to the eccentricities of grown-ups we were not a little surprised and even intrigued by this. I asked Lizzie, as the most reliable source of information, what she thought about this to which she replied diplomatically, 'Your Uncle John is sometimes a law unto hissel'.

Sadly, as I was to learn much later, uncle's eccentricities were the first symptoms of a mental disease known as *dementia praecox*. Back at Trinity the following term, where his main claim to fame was as Master of Foot Beagles, his 'eccentricities' became ever more pronounced. There was an incident, I never knew exactly what, which caused the College authorities to call in medical advice and he was pronounced insane.

Granny was informed. Page was sent for and ordered that the car be made ready within half an hour to drive to London. The journey was completed, stopping only for petrol on the way, in a little under twelve hours. A quite remarkable feat in those days. During the whole journey Granny sat bolt upright in the back seat without uttering a single word. Having seen the specialists and learning that John had to be committed to a lunatic asylum, Page climbed back into the driver's seat and drove her all the way back to Kinloch.

John was eventually transferred to what was then a private asylum, Crichton Homes in Dumfries where he was to remain for the rest of his life. As for Granny she never accepted that advances in medical science would not in time produce a cure. During her lifetime none of Uncle John's possessions at Kinloch was to be touched and she lived in the belief that any day he might walk through the door again. She died in 1942 when she was well into her eighties and left the entire estate to her son with the strict instruction that nothing was to be altered or sold whilst he was alive. It was to remain a time capsule until Uncle John finally died in 1971.

As for my brother and me, when the New Year of 1925 dawned the prospects looked set fair for a long and happy life ahead with little to concern us save the netting of rabbits and the catching of enormous pike.

Little did we know that the mysterious comings and goings of our mother which we had observed during our time at Kinloch were in fact house hunting excursions to find the home where we were destined to spend most of the rest of our childhood years.

CHAPTER FOUR

Alas regardless of their doom,
The little victims play!
No sense have they of ills to come,
Nor care beyond to-day.
Ode on a Distant Prospect of Eton College
Thomas Gray

Little was I to know, as the inter-island steamer pulled away from Stronsay's shores, leaving my father standing desolately at the pier-head that I was destined not to return for many years. The decisions had, however, already been made and the die cast. Mountpleasant and everything with it was to be sold and the family was to emigrate to Scotland where it was planned to buy a farm.

It was only many years afterwards that I was to hear an account of Dad's rearguard action at Mountpleasant. Whilst it is true that Mum, after the first flush of romantic fervour at being carried off by her handsome lover to a love nest created for her on a remote storm-tossed island, found the storm-tossing a bit much and the social life a trifle scanty, there were other considerations to the decision to move south. One of the chief of these was that my brother and I were required to be educated. This was something which, when I first heard mention of it, filled me with a mixture of horror mixed with terror. Gordon was afflicted with the same thing to an even greater degree.

There was, I might say, a perfectly good dame's school on Stronsay and a quite excellent Academy in Kirkwall for anyone who might want educating beyond the three Rs of reading, writing and arithmetic but this was not considered to be good enough for us. Why we should have been elected by fate to be dispatched at an early age to a monastic boarding establishment was very far from clear to us but that was the way it was. To travel to and fro three times a year, entailing a journey lasting three days each way, weather permitting, was not regarded as a practical proposition. The answer was to move the mountain nearer to Mahommet.

I do not think that Dad found this altogether unwelcome but he did, apparently, find the disposal of his part of the island a depressing, not to say tiresome, business. Land in the Orkneys was not at that time a particularly bullish market and Mountpleasant a positive drug.

It was Harriet Hourston herself who was years afterwards to tell me how it all finished up.

Apparently Father was sitting gloomily in front of the fire in the drawing room when, seized with a sudden impulse, he rang the bell furiously for the only retainer left to him who was Harriet. The following conversation then took place:

'Harriet, I hear you are going to get married.'

'Yes indeed, Captain.'

'Have you got a house?'

'No, we havn't found a house yet, Captain.'

'Why don't you have this one?'

'You are joking, Captain.'

But the Captain, as everyone knew him on the island, was not joking. A price of one hundred pounds was fixed. Three days later he piled his bags into the back of the open Sunbeam tourer and caught the steamer for Kirkwall, never to be seen on his native island again. Everything else was left at Mountpleasant down to the last teaspoon and tiger skin rugs (with which the house abounded).

Harriet, who married the island roadman, continued to live at Mountpleasant for a further forty years, only retiring to Kirkwall after her husband died. Shortly before she left I had returned to Stronsay with my wife to write a book*. One of the first things we did was to drive out to Mountpleasant. As we stood looking over the garden wall wondering if we dared call without warning, Harriet appeared.

'I ken fine who you are' she called, 'Come awa' ben.' It was a strange feeling to be shown over the house again after so many years. Hardly anything could have been moved. The tiger skin rugs were still on the highly polished floor and our cots still by the window in the night nursery, looking out over St Catherine's Bay and Harriet and her husband still slept in the room off the kitchen where she had always slept. There was not a spot of dust nor an unpolished surface anywhere. *Sic transit gloria mundi*.

But now for Gordon and I at Kinloch, our time was up. Another transformation scene in the pantomime was about to take place.

By some strange omission in the banking of memories I do not now have any recollection of the actual process of migration from Granny's house, Wester Kinloch, to what was to be our new home, Tullochford near Old Meldrum in Aberdeenshire. It was as if one night I had gone to bed as usual in my room overlooking the rockwalls at Kinloch and the next morning awoken in the bedroom I was to share with my brother which looked out over the farm steading at Tullochford. Certainly that night was a memorable one as I shall relate.

Our bedroom was one the first floor. As usual when it came to time for lights out, the curtains were drawn and the windows opened so that we would benefit from what was then regarded as the surest recipe for all good health, plenty of fresh air. Scarcely could I have fallen, as was my wont, into immediate and profound slumber than I became sleepily conscious of what I can only describe as plopping noises from the direction of the window and of a body or bodies landing on the quilt of my bed. 'Don't worry, it's only a cat' I remember Gordon in the next bed whispering, before lapsing back into my deep sleep.

The following morning when our new governess came in to draw the curtains, I awoke sharply enough when she gave a sort

* *Against the Wind*, Heinemann, 1964

of strangled scream. There was not one or even two cats in the room. There must have been over twenty of them. They were on my bed, on Gordon's bed, occupying all the chairs or just curled up on the carpet. It must simply have been raining cats all night. I can remember being totally delighted by this invasion but the world of grown-ups took a quite different view.

The explanation of this phenomenon lay with the previous owner of the farm who had been a life-long bachelor of rather reclusive habits, and whose bedroom it was that we occupied. I do not know if he was a particularly dedicated cat lover in the true sense or simply that he had made no conscious efforts over the years to control the abandoned breeding habits of the farmyard cats which are part and parcel of the livestock of any farm. Either way the cats which had curled up in our bedroom that night were to prove to be only a handful of the most privileged amongst a vast cat population which overran every nook and cranny of the farm steading. How this problem was ultimately overcome I do not now remember but certainly we were to sleep with our bedroom window shut for many weeks to come.

By the standards of those days, Tullochford was quite a large farm. It consisted of just over three hundred acres of prime agricultural land in the heart of some of the finest agricultural land in Scotland. Aberdeenshire is famed throughout the world for the quality of its beef and Aberdeen Angus cattle are ambassadors of quality to the farthest flung corners of the globe.

Tullochford, before father had bought it, had been a dairy farm and he intended to carry on the tradition. In the 1920s agriculture was still in the age of the horse with mechanisation not to come for many years. All the tilling of the fields and the harvesting of the crops was by horse power. There was as yet no electricity on the farm and all the water for domestic or farm use was pumped by our own windmill on the principle of no wind, no water. The threshing mill was driven by a water wheel powered by water from the mill dam. On threshing days the sluice gate would be raised and the water race down the mill lade to start the great wheel turning which in turn brought the engine to life with much clattering and clanking.

After the, for us, almost unreal interlude at Granny's house where at a touch of a switch the rooms were flooded with light, it was back to the island days of oil lamps and candles to light us to bed. There was only one department where we stole a march on our neighbours which was that we had a telephone. It was one of those black standard upright affairs where you jigged the receiver up and down endlessly to attract the attention of the operator. The telephone number was Old Meldrum 2, Old Meldrum 1 being the Post Office itself. The directory listing the numbers of other subscribers was contained on one side of a small card.

The farm house itself was, as was usual with most of the neighbouring farms, quite large designed as they were to accommodate the large families traditional amongst the farming communities and, to our young eyes, although only on two stories, immensely tall and gaunt with high sloping roofs and stark chimney stacks. There were in fact only seven bedrooms with sundry living rooms but its most striking feature was the immense stone-flagged kitchen off which opened all manner of supporting rooms like larders, a still-room store-rooms and laundry rooms and sculleries. The kitchen with its great burnished stove and twenty foot scrubbed-white table was the very heart of the house and the centre round which everything revolved.

It was no time at all before Gordon and I became totally involved in our new life. I might go further and say that we both positively embraced it. It was really a case, as the French put it so well, of *plus ça change, plus c'est la meme chose*. For us the magic continued. It was only a different sort of magic.

The whims and vagaries of the grown-ups who controlled our destiny were beyond our comprehension and totally beyond our power of influence. The real things in our lives were everyday things like the total reliability of the changing of the seasons. The sun rose and the sun set with commendable regularity. Each day was a new adventure of exploration in which the grown-up world had little part. Where our lives at Mountpleasant had been dominated by the winds and the tides and the natural life of the bird population and the creatures of the sea, life at Wester Kinloch, for all the wonders of sophisticated living for us to marvel at, had been far more exciting because of the woods and the trees to climb, the cock pheasants strutting on the lawns and the wild geese tumbling down in their thousands out of the skies. Now, at Tullochford, whole new magical vistas had opened up with all the pulsating life of the farmyard on our doorstep and the tilled fields stretching away to unexplored horizons.

Tullochford may have been a dairy farm with a herd of forty Friesian milking cows and their followers but it was the stables which for us was the most irresistable attraction. The 'working strength' consisted of six great Clydesdale mares and it was round them that the whole social hierarchy revolved. The horses worked in pairs and each pair was the responsibility of the first, second and third horseman in the strictest order of seniority. It was the first horseman and his pair which led the way out of the stables to work at first light in the morning and who set the pace throughout the working day whether it be ploughing, harrowing, rolling or any other of the daily tasks with the pairs of the second and third horsemen echeloned behind him. The horsemen were the aristocracy of the farm yard with only the head cattleman rating anywhere beside them in the social tree. There were also sundry dogsbodies, farm boys of thirteen or fourteen years old who rated nowhere at all. These loons or 'orra-men' as they were called, were serving their apprenticeship as farm workers and were paid something in the region of ten pounds a year, six-monthly in arrears and lived in the bothy with the other single men. No farm worker had more than one day's holiday a year, New Year's Day, and that only started after the needs of whatever animals were in their charge had been attended to and ended when they had to be 'bedded' at night.

To modern eyes the lot of the farm worker in those days must seem to have been the closest thing to slavery but it was a far call indeed from the 'dark, satanic mills' of William Blake. For me at the age of five, going on six, I could imagine no more perfect existence nor a higher ambition in life than to become a first horseman.

The farm worker's day was immutably sign-posted by the clock; six in the morning, twelve midday and six o'clock in the evening. At six in the morning all the single men who lived a communal life in the bothy had their breakfast served in the house, seated round the big scrubbed table in the kitchen. It consisted of the same ingredients every day. A large plate of brose which was simply raw oatmeal scalded in water and hunks of freshly baked bread with butter. Jam was reserved for special occasions just as in exceptionally cold weather, a tot of whisky was added to the brose.

At midday and at six in the evening the bothy meals were the responsibility of the grieve's wife who lived in one of the tied cottar houses provided for married farm workers. The grieve was the overall boss of all farming activities and a man of considerable stature and power. Not very long after Dad bought the farm, he was taken severely to task by a neighbouring farmer for paying his grieve the quite unheard of sum of £100 a year.

'Ma Gawd! Ma Gawd! Captain ye'll be the ruin of us 'a paying a grieve sic an' extrrraaavagant amount of sillar,' complained John Strachan of Crichie, one of the most renowned of all Aberdeenshire farmers at the time.

Jimmy Pratt, the grieve in question, was a man of great dignity who took his family to church on Sundays wearing a well-pressed blue suit but on weekdays was in shirtsleeves working alongside his men. In addition to the great sum of a hundred pounds a year he had, in common with other married workers in tied cottages, free coal as well as free oatmeal and milk and a patch of garden where he could grow his own vegetables. Most evening he would sit with our father in his study discussing the rotation of crops, the market prices and other weighty matters. His power as head executive on the ground, as it were, was absolute.

The routine of the household was also governed absolutely by the clock. Gordon and I had breakast on our own in the downstairs dining room at eight o'clock. Two hours of lessons in the nursery upstairs, followed by a supervised walk after which we could run free for the rest of the day, subject only to nursery lunch (downstairs on Sunday after church). Bath time was six o'clock followed by supper upstairs with bed at seven-thirty and candles snuffed out at eight. Although this may sound a painfully dull routine to the modern child with regular treats and surprises organised by the parents to distract from a diet of videos and television we, not having any option, did not find it so at all.

Nor is it to say that our parents were not indulgent or showed any lack of interest in our upbringing. Soon we had so many interests to occupy us that the days were not nearly long enough. One of their indulgences was when we were each bought beehives which were set side by side down in the vegetable garden. Not only hives, each with its resident swarm of bees but all the paraphernalia of the bee-keeper's art. Masks and protective clothing, smokers to control the infuriated bees when we removed the tops of their hives to inspect the progress of their honey-making activities and additional sections to impose one on top of the other as their productivity increased beyond the capacity of the original frame – hopefully.

It need hardly be remarked that this stirred up the ever-present competitive spirit between Gordon and me to a very high pitch indeed. When the warming sun of springtime stirred the bees out of their long winter sleep, we would sit, each crouched alongside our own hives to watch the batallions of bees setting forth in search of blossom from which to fill their tiny sacs with honey to be borne back to the hive. Nor need it be remarked that, with the history of my fortunes in competition with Gordon on Stronsay fresh in mind, it was not long before it became blindingly obvious that the traffic from my hive was much more sparse than it was from Gordon's where the comings and goings of his bees soon reached almost congestion point. That first summer I watched with nail-biting fury amounting almost to neurosis as he added storey after storey to his hive whilst mine never rose above the first floor. To this day I can offer no explanation why the loving care I lavished on my bees was not returned in like measure whilst Gordon's flourished mightily in response to what I considered to be his much more cavalier attitude.

There was another activity, however, in which I was not to fare so badly by comparison. One of Dad's 'improvements' to the existing farm steading was the building of a very large pig house. This occupied one whole side of the steading and, in addition to its pig-rearing function, had the added advantage of blocking off the midden from the house from which it had only been separated previously by a narrow farm road and a low wall.

As part of Dad's campaign to inspire in us a profit-making incentive and so turn us eventually into useful citizens, he had the idea that we should go in for rabbit keeping. These were not to be just any old bunnies to be kept in a hutch and fed on carrots and lettuce. He had read in one of his farming magazines that there was a comparatively new and fashionable breed of rabbit called a Blue Bevern from which great profits could be made in the arcane world of rabbit breeding although whether as meat or breeding stock was not immediately clear. Anyway it was an idea into which we entered with the greatest of enthusiasm. The pig house had been divided into a number of quite large pens to accommodate breeding sows and initially Gordon and I were to be alloted one of these pens each. Excitement reached fever pitch when the first two pairs of breeding rabbits arrived and were installed each in their own pens in accommodation which rivalled in its facilities that of a first class hotel in terms of Bunnyland. The expression 'to breed like rabbits' is not a vain one and it was no time at all before the evidence of the approach of motherhood in both does was unmistakably apparent. The two bucks were then moved to share one pen as bachelor accommodation whilst the other was turned into a pre-natal clinic. Then, within what seemed like a remarkably short space of time, first Gordon's doe (of course) gave birth to a litter, followed by mine a few days later. However Fate was to intervene between the two events. When the litter to Gordon's doe was born he immediately had them all out of the breeding hutch to be counted and gloated upon. The following morning when, not even waiting for breakfast, he went out to repeat this act of one-upmanship the nest was bare. Mother Rabbit had eaten the lot – all six of them. This is a common enough occurrence if the doe is upset too soon after the birth. Well warned by this disaster when my litter arrived forty-eight hours later I stayed well clear and very soon afterwards I had little rabbits hopping around all over the place. In an indecently short space of time the whole maternal cycle had started all over again.

It was not long before the rabbit breeding business started to take off in a big way which resulted in my demanding more and more *lebensraum* for my flock, reluctantly conceded by Dad at the expense of his pigs. However Gordon's fortunes never flourished in the same way. He became dreadfully piqued by this. Finally his distress was such that he went out of rabbits and took up breeding guinea pigs instead. Although it is true that guinea pigs reproduce themselves at an even more impossibly high rate than rabbits, this was not a sound financial move on his part. Whilst I managed to do an admittedly small amount of trading in my rabbits his guinea pigs proved to be a complete drug on the market.

Important and all-absorbing as these matters undoubtedly were, there fell, at the zenith of that summer of 1926, a shadow across our young lives of such depths as to be almost indescribable. It happened in the most casual possible way. One morning, shortly after breakfast our mother made the announcement that we would all be going to Aberdeen the following day to have Gordon fitted out for his school clothes. School clothes!

This matter of our being eventually sent away to school had long been hovering about somewhere below the immediate horizon. It had however so lacked definition as to be part of a never-never land. It was just like those stories on which we had so far been brought up, all of which seemed to start with 'once upon a time.'

The idea of being banished to a foreign world far removed from everything that was familiar and trusted was something that was almost beyond our comprehension. To be thrown in with a lot of other boys of our own age was an intimidating prospect indeed.

When this blow finally fell we had only been to Aberdeen, which was twenty miles away, a handful of times. It was, of course, inclined to be awe-inspiring to be suddenly released into a world where so many men and women hurried to and fro, jostling each other on the pavements and with cars whizzing up and down the streets all the time. Particularly impressive were the tram cars which rattled and banged along on their rails set in the cobbled roadway and onto which some people sprang with a sophisticated insouciance whilst, at each stop, others dropped off to go scurrying about their pedestrian business. What sort of business that might be I had no idea.

This visit to Aberdeen was however to be doubly memorable. Not only was the business of buying school clothes a considerable excitement but there was a treat planned for the afternoon which put even that in the shade. We were to be taken to the cinema.

The cinema was, in those days, usually referred to as the 'moving pictures' or by those who were bang up-to-date with the jargon of the day as the 'movies'. It was before the days of the 'talking pictures', except perhaps in the larger centres of civilisation, and which were known as the 'talkies'. With only our single experience of Mr Mackay's magic lantern show in Orkney to go by we had very little idea of what to expect but whatever it was it exceeded our wildest imaginings.

The picture we saw was that great classic, the silent version of *Ben Hur*. Although we had nothing to compare it with, I believe that *Ben Hur* crossed new frontiers on the film maker's art. We sat glued to our seats and when, at the climax of the great chariot race, the galloping horses and the chariots appeared to roar out of the picture right over the heads of the audience, everyone screamed and ducked down in their seats in terrified delight. I was not to see another picture for a further two years by which time the 'talkies' had become firmly established. This was *Dracula* and it filled me, as it did the whole nation, with real terror. I had the most terrible nightmares for a long time afterwards, peopled with fearful bat-like figures and hideous with the groans of corpses having stakes driven into their hearts. These two great experiences made up the total of my cinema going until I was in my late teens. In these days of saturation television and the deifying of the international stars of the silver screen this may seem to be verging on the quaint but I cannot say that it has ever made me feel particularly deprived in my upbringing. Indeed many of my contemporaries could not match even my record of cinema attendances.

Gordon's final dispatching to his preparatory school took place in September when the trees were still in leaf and the months before his promised release in the week before Christmas must have seemed an eternity ahead. Such was the importance of the occasion that Dad decreed that we should all drive to the school to see to his final immolation.

Alton Burn which was the name of the institution to be charged with our further education stood on the bleak shores of the Moray Firth about a mile outside the northerly holiday resort of Nairn which in turn is some twelve miles from Inverness at the top end of the Caledonian Canal. To make this long expedition of about a hundred miles by motor-car was quite an undertaking. I do not know what had happened to Dad's splendid open Sunbeam tourer – rumour had it that he had given it away to a bystander on the pier at Whitehall when he had finally left Stronsay – but he had since acquired an Austin Sixteen. This was a staid upright sort of car with running boards, one of which accommodated a red, two-gallon spare can of petrol and was considered by one and all to be quite some motor-car. There was even a six-inch square window, set in the roof, which you could push upwards when the weather was sufficiently clement so as to admit a refreshing draught of air.

Father was a steady driver who proceeded at his set speed of somewhere between twenty and twenty-five miles an hour and which could sometimes rise, when the road could be seen to stretch straight ahead for some distance, to almost thirty. He very much disliked anything to impede his progress so that when any sort of obstacle loomed ahead he would sound his horn loudly and repeatedly which was achieved by pumping a large rubber bulb attached to something rather like a hunting horn on the outside of the vehicle. He would never, however, slacken speed. His attitude was 'Get out of my way, damn you, or I'll run you over.' This was apt to make driving with father a tense business despite his indisputable cautiousness. Nor were long car journeys made any easier for me on account of a tendency to car-sickness. This was also something which was not permitted to impede progress with the result that I would spend most of the journey with my head stuck out of the window.

There was also the constant risk of breakdown. This was usually as a result of a puncture. Then it would be a matter of all hands on deck as the car was precariously jacked up, nuts and bolts striven with and rather surprised congratulations all round when the emergency had been successfully dealt with. As the roads in those days were still very rough and tyres with their inner tubes still in a primitive stage of development, punctures were in the region of probability on a hundred-mile trip and to be reckoned with in estimating a possible time of arrival. There were also planned stops for luncheon and tea so that that the undertaking consumed a whole day, followed by a night in an hotel in Nairn with the next day devoted to the return journey.

The Headmaster of Alton Burn was a Major N.G. Pearson M.C., M.A., fellow officer of Dad's in the Gordon Highlanders during the 1914–18 War. He had bought the school, rather like other officers who had gone in for chicken farming or other ventures after their discharge, to eke out a slender income and he ran it with his wife, Lucy, who had the reputation of being very musical.

To a small boy in short trousers, worn out after an interminable car-sick journey, N.G. (as he was universally known) presented a formidable figure indeed. He was a large man of military bearing with a florid complexion which looked as if it might at any moment explode into a bright sunset-red. His wife, Lucy, by contrast, was thin, flat-breasted and paper-white. The drawing room into which we were shown was dominated by a grand piano on a raised dais set around by music stands, as if at any moment one might be expected to leap up and take part in an impromptu concert.

The grown-ups were being indulged in small glasses of dry sherry when N.G., apparently recollecting what we were there for, suddenly turned to Gordon and said, 'Ah, Sutherland, you'll probably want to join the others for their evening mug of cocoa, so you had better say your good-byes and cut along now.'

At that he pressed a bell and a body appeared who, after Gordon had been allowed a perfunctory peck on the cheek all round, whisked him away to unknown regions. It was only when we were driving back to our hotel in Nairn that I noticed that Mum in the front seat was sobbing quietly into her handkerchief whilst Dad gripped the steering wheel and stared steadfastly forward into the gathering dusk.

Although this brief preview of what the Fates had in store for me did not do very much to assure me that I was going to live happily ever after, it did at least do something towards allaying the fear of the unknown, surely the most debilitating of all forms of fear. At least now I had had a glimpse of the enemy. At the same time it made me cling to the security of life on the farm with even greater intensity.

It was an almost tangible pleasure to waken early in my bed under the night nursery window and listen to the sounds of the day beginning. First there would be the sounds of the farm workers' tacked boots as they made their way along the side of the house for their breakfast of brose and steaming mugs of black tea in the kitchen below. Quite often there may have been a cow in the byre, in the first pangs of calving, lowing at intervals through the night. Now the others would join in, at the first clanking of pails, waiting impatiently for their turn to come to be milked. In those early days all the milking was done by hand although Dad was later to be one of the first to install a milking machine. Milking, as I was soon to learn, was quite a tricky business mainly because of the willfulness of the cows rather than anything else. A cow, having got used to the hand of her regular milker, would only tolerate another with the greatest reluctance. By spitefully contracting the muscles of its udders it could hold back on the flow of its milk in the most exasperating way. The beginner should also beware lest with a vicious swing of its tail he or she be caught an almighty swipe around the ears, an experience which, especially with a wet tail, could be very far from pleasant.

It would not be long before the arrival of the pig-man with their morning feed would bring on an outbreak of such squealing as to waken the dead and shortly after that, as the sun first started to lighten the sky, the horses could be heard stamping their great iron-clad hooves, impatient to set off for the days' work in the fields.

Without Gordon to squabble and compete with, the months before Christmas might, despite all the activity going on around me, have weighed heavy on my hands had I not inherited the responsibility for looking after his already obscenely large and rapidly multiplying flock of guinea pigs and that of dealing with the autumnal harvest of his industrious hive of bees. Removing the great number of combs they had produced to be stored on the cool slate slabs of the house dairy was some compensation for the deplorable performance of my own hive. I really don't think I could have stood his gloating had he been there in person. Then there were red-letter days on the farm, such as a day on which a stack of corn was to be thrashed.

When the harvest was brought in, the sheaves of corn were built into stacks, each stack consisting of perhaps a dozen or more cartloads brought in from the fields where they had been standing in stooks. The crops in those days were, of course, cut by a horse-drawn binder which tossed out the bound sheaves for the gang of stookers coming behind. It was the great festival of the year and as far removed from the modern harvesting scene with its vast combine harvesters as it is possible to imagine.

The stack yards with the stacks standing in serried ranks were the outward and visible testimony of how the general efficiency of each individual farm was to be judged by the passer-by – and, even more critically, by the nearest neighbours. A good stack builder was a pearl beyond price who could impose on any stack he built a character as individual as a personal signature. Not only had the stack to be as perfectly symmetrical as ingenuity and experience could provide but it had to be thatched against the weather and in the neatness of the thatching, down to the top-knot which rounded it off, the whole world sat in judgement.

Every farm of any size had its own threshing mill which was usually driven like ours by a water wheel, powered by water from the mill dam. On threshing days the sluice gate of the dam would be opened to allow the water to race down the mill lade to get the wheel turning and the engine in the engine house clanking and to set the thresher itself with its sharp blades whizzing round at an astonishing speed. But before all this operation was put in motion there came almost the most exciting part of the whole thing which was the demolition of the stack in the stack yard.

As the sheaves were forked down to be carried off to the mill and the level of the stack started to get lower and lower, the excitement mounted. The dogs prowled round ominously with their ears cocked and their hackles bristling and the bystanders had their stout sticks raised at the ready. The first rats, great brown monsters with their long scaly tails, would make a dash for it when there were quite a lot of sheaves still to go but it was when it got down to the last few that the hunt started to get really furious. With each one of the last sheaves to be lifted from the stony base of the stack a veritable wave of rats was likely to erupt to be fallen upon by the waiting vigilantes. A rat, out in the open with no place to turn for refuge, is vulnerable indeed, but they do not lack in guile. With the odds set heavily against them, there were not a few which did, nevertheless, make good their escape to fight again another day. The war against the rats on the farm was unrelenting.

Christmas in those far-off days was not a festival which was much celebrated in Scotland. Certainly in the country areas it was not even declared a holiday. Whereas in England Christmas has traditionally always been given the full treatment with an abundance of robins, mistletoe and usually non-existent snow, in Scotland all the real festivities were, and in many places still are, reserved for the bringing in of the New Year. Of course now the two celebrations are merged into one in both countries so that everything in the business and social world comes to an abrupt stop some days in advance of 25 December and hostilities are not again formally resumed until some time in January. But this was not always so.

I do not now remember any of the Christmases of my childhood very clearly although there was the episode of the figs recounted earlier. Certainly there were no festivities on the scale that children have the right to expect nowadays. The only thing I can remember, and still with a tremor of excitement, is the opening of Christmas stockings, most carefully and lovingly prepared and smuggled, supposedly long after we were deemed to be fast asleep, into our bedroom to be hung on a bedpost. With a tangerine in the toe and two crackers stuck out of the top, the contents in between – penny whistles, chocolate money, small puzzle games and other items of ineffable delight – brought forth gasps of wonder. For the rest I can recall little of Christmases past except the ceremonial lighting of the Christmas pudding soaked in brandy which was Dad's special responsibility and the pulling of crackers round the table at the end of Christmas lunch. There was certainly no elaborately decorated Christmas tree nor a ceremonial present-giving ceremony such as is the universal practice today.

In fact present-giving of any sort at specific seasons of the year never loomed very large in our calendar so far as I can now recollect it was something to be passionately looked forward to. Birthdays, in particular, were pretty well non-events. Yet this is something in which my memory may be at fault. When, many years after the years of my childhood on Stronsay, my wife, Diana, and I returned for a long visit, a contemporary of those days said that the only thing about my brother and I that he could remember clearly was the splendour of the toys we had to play with and the elaborate parties given for us by our parents to which one and all were invited. Maybe there is some sort of psychological block there somewhere.

Gordon got back from Alton Burn for the Christmas holidays looking pale and fed up. He rallied a bit when he inspected his stock of guinea pigs which in his three months' absence had almost doubled in numbers and were now seriously threatening to over-run the whole of the piggery and he was greatly gratified to view his stock of honey combs. Other than that he did not have a great deal to say. All that I really gathered about school was that he did not like it. There was rather a bad moment when, early in January, his school report arrived. These reports on one's progress or otherwise in the past term which were to dog us for many years to come, were very elaborate. Each subject was reported upon in the greatest detail by the master or mistress concerned. Place in class was shown, together with the names and ages of the other boys in the class and their comparative achievements. Age was a factor which was always considered a matter of great import. Thus, if a boy of seven years and two months had gained a higher mark in geography than a boy of seven years and eight months, it was a matter of great satisfaction for the parents. If, on the other hand, the positions were reversed, it amounted to something on which one felt some sort of court of enquiry should be convened.

At the bottom of the report came the headmaster's summing-up, which covered everything from school work to games and outside activities and including 'attitudes'. As Gordon had come firmly bottom in every school subject except games in which he was described as showing promise, N.G.'s comments are not hard to imagine. They were summed up in one final sentence which read: 'This boy must learn to stop staring out of the window whilst lessons are in progress.'

This ferocious indictment of their first born's mental capabilities produced a surprisingly mild reaction on the part of the parents. The only thing that caused Dad to give a brief snort of irritation was when he came to examine the list of the term's extras as well as the account to be paid in advance for the following term which had been enclosed, one cannot but feel rather tactlessly, in the package.

Shortly after Gordon had returned for the spring term to Alton Burn, there occurred an event which took me completely by surprise. Mum had a baby. It is perhaps as good an indication as any of the generation gap which existed in our family and which was regarded in those times as perfectly normal, that such a momentous event should not have been considered as worth mentioning as being in prospect. Certainly the life our parents lived was completely remote from ours. We were vaguely conscious that they were very social with a wide and increasing circle of friends of which we had no part whilst we were equally absorbed in our own doings in which they only took a kindly but Olympian interest. The small triumphs and the bruises and bumps of our daily lives were really our own affair or the concern of those appointed to look after us.

But to go back to Mum's baby. I suppose I must have been vaguely aware of her changing shape and decreasing activeness but there was no way in which I could have related this to the process of procreation which was going on around me the whole time and with which I was so familiar. Yet I must have had *some* inkling.

The baby, who turned out to be my younger brother John, was born about mid-morning on the last day of January. I can remember the moment perfectly. I was playing about on my own in front of the house when Doctor Greig arrived in his pony and trap. This was always quite an event in itself.

Doctor Greig was about eighty years old and I suppose one of the last, if not the very last, to use a horse and trap to go about his daily business. He lived in a tiny picturesque cottage on the banks of the river Ythan, near Fyvie, which was five miles away. He had lived in his cottage, which did not even have running water, ever since he had set up in practice almost sixty years earlier. He was everything one would expect of a solid Victorian professional gentleman. He had a large impressive white beard, a gruff manner belied by a twinkle in the eye and a seemingly inexhaustible supply of peppermints which he distributed from a pocket in the mysterious folds of his Gladstone cape to any child who might cross his path in the course of his daily rounds. He drove his open trap in all weathers and in winter would think nothing of plunging waist-high through snow drifts to reach a marooned patient.

The doctor also always carried with him the traditional little black bag containing all his medical paraphernalia and this has given rise to a story about the arrival of my brother John which I can only hope is apocryphal. There was an alternative to the traditional answer of 'under a gooseberry bush' to the question of where babies came from which was 'out of the doctor's little black bag'. It is related that when Doctor Greig arrived for the birth to find me moodily kicking a stone about in front of the house, he held up his little black bag and said: 'And what do you suppose I have got in my little black bag?' To which I am said to have replied. 'I expect it is only a baby' and went on kicking my stone. Can I have been such a ghastly precocious little monster? I sometimes suspect I might have been.

There was a by-product of the birth of brother John which was to prove a bonus of great worth. A week or so before the expected date of arrival there had been a new addition to the staff whom we were instructed to address as Nurse Webster. She was a tall and angular lady who, at the time of her arrival, appeared to have no particular function in relation to our own lives. I cannot remember now who was in charge of Gordon and me at the time. She was just one of a succession of, in our view, totally unsatisfactory ladies who had come and gone at irregular intervals and who filled the titular role of Nanny. Since the days of our much-loved Miss Johnstone at Mountpleasant and our friend and counsellor at Kinloch, Lizzie, the ladies who had filled this uncongenial role had only been distinctive to the degree in which we had disliked them. One of the best, in my recollection, had been a nice, giggly girl who let us do more or less whatever we wanted. Alas, her complaisance had proved to be her downfall. Her brief reign had been during the time when we were at Kinloch. It appeared that the terms of her employment were that she had one night off a week but she was only allowed to relinquish her duties after we had been tucked up in bed and were safely asleep. The time when we could be deemed to be safely asleep was in the nature of being a fairly moveable feast.

Apparently it was her custom, if we were being unusually fractious, to turn on the gas fire in our bedroom and neglect to light it. Then, when we had been rendered unconscious, turn off the gas, leap onto her bicycle and speed off to keep her assignation with her beau. On this occasion such had been the pressing nature of her engagement that she neglected to turn off the gas before making her escape. By some misfortune for her, or good fortune for us, my mother had thought to come up to our room to make sure that all was well. It can also be said that it was only by the greatest of good fortune that, when she opened our bedroom door she was not, unusually for her, smoking a cigarette at the time.

By contrast one of the more despotic of our minders proved to be so intolerable that we were driven to a state of open revolution. The situation was so bad that she was driven to complain to Mum.

'Why,' I can remember my mother chiding us 'are you so beastly to Miss X?' The answer came to me in a flash of rare inspiration.

'Because, Mummy' I said, opening my honest blue eyes, 'she is always saying such nasty things about you!'

The following morning the unfortunate lady found herself,

with her trunk packed, being driven to the nearest railway station.

The bonus to which I have referred, following my mother's accouchment, was that Nurse Webster was taken onto the permanent staff as nurse for the infant John with the additional responsibility of looking after me. She was to prove one of the most formative influences in my life until it came my turn to be sent off to Alton Burn and, after that, to be the single person on whom I could rely and from whom I had no secrets.

If I have given the impression that Tullochford was a very grand household where we were surrounded by servants and cossetted in the same way as we had been under Granny's regime at Kinloch, nothing could be further from the case.

Tullochford was a most ordinary house and, although large by more modern standards, typical of the average Aberdeenshire farmhouse on a reasonably large farm. It should be remembered that in those days even the most modest of middle class families had servants. The Industrial Revolution of the nineteenth century had seen the country changing from being an entirely agricultural economy to becoming the greatest industrial power in the world with the consequent shifting of labour from the countryside into the mills and factories of the cities but, in the 1920s and 30s, the single greatest employment was still in domestic service. Thus to have a cook and a couple of housemaids in a household was not any sign of high social status or some prosperity. Nor did being brought up on a farm as the farmer's son lend itself to any form of pretension.

At the same time there was really no such thing in those days as what is nowadays described as a 'gentlemen farmer'. A landowner let his lands to tenants and lived, sometimes rather precariously let it be said, in 'the big house' off the proceeds. That he might farm any part of his lands himself would never have occurred to him. He did however preserve his exclusive *droit de seigneur* to shoot the game on his lands and catch the fish in his own waters should he be lucky enough to own any. At the same time there was no more democratic relationship on earth than that enjoyed by a landowner in the old feudal tradition and his tenants. With Dad farming his own land himself, it did leave us in the social hierarchy as neither fish, flesh nor fowl, not that this worried us one iota. It was something that never crossed our minds.

My greatest friend at the time I am now talking about was 'Jocky' Pratt, who was the son of Jimmy Pratt, the farm grieve. Jock was a year older than me and went daily to the local school at Bartle Chapel which was something like three miles away. He and his younger brother Billy walked there every day with their 'piece', usually a cheese sandwich, in their school satchels and trudged or, rather, ran back again in the afternoon. He shared with me a total bewilderment that I was not to be allowed to do the same thing and he listened in total unbelief to tales of what might be in store for me.

Jocky was the best of companions and we spent whatever time he was not at school in each other's company. He knew every hedge and ditch on the farm as well as far beyond. More importantly from my point of view he was an expert on the wild bird and animal life. Whilst it amazed me that he had never seen a puffin or knew what a gullery was like in nesting time, he was equally astonished that I did not recognise a partridge or a bird as common as a wood pigeon. An island like Stronsay with no trees or even proper hedges was something he found hard to take in but it was nothing to my incredulity when he told me he had never seen the sea.

It was with Jocky that first spring that I first discovered the ineffable delight of bird nesting. I don't suppose there was a country boy in those days who did not look forward to bird nesting. On the island where you could not walk in some places without danger of treading on a nest of eggs, the joy of discovering a lark's nest or a clutch of partridge's eggs hidden in the remote corner of a field was quite a different more exciting matter.

I suppose that nowadays to lay claim to being a bird's egg collector would be to invite all manner of abuse from well-meaning people devoted to the protection of everything but what they are going on about is something quite different. There is a world of difference between professional egg thieves raiding the nests of rare breeds of birds to satisfy the greed of collectors and the schoolboy enthusiast.

The most rewarding hunting grounds for us were the hedges and bushes (like rhodendrons) much favoured by such birds as thrushes and blackbirds but there were others, particularly the tree nesting birds, which presented a much greater challenge. To climb up to a pigeon's nest in a comparatively low fir tree was not always all that easy but to reach a crow's nest up in the thin branches of much taller trees was a tricky business indeed. So much so that there was a complete parental interdict against even trying. Of course the object of bird nesting was not wantonly to rob the nests. After all once you had got a blackbird's egg in your collection you did not want a dozen. Nonetheless to know where all the blackbirds' nests were and to watch the success of the hatching out was highly satisfactory. To discover the nests of rarer birds like a wren or the great variety of tits was the cream on the cake and the most elaborate care was taken to see that they should not be disturbed.

Then there were all sorts of animals which were quite new to me. I had never for instance seen a hedgehog or a mole and could not tell the difference between a stoat and a weasel and something like a squirrel was a creature to be wondered at.

Then there were the walks with my new found friend, Nurse Webster, taking turns to push my pink little new brother in his pram. The thing which was to me, at the age of six, so extraordinary was that Nurse Webster (as with Miss Johnstone, I never got to know her first name) talked to me of all manner of things, as if I were at least a little more grown up. She was a qualified nurse – an S.R.N., or the equivalent – and had travelled far and wide including working in a hospital in the 1914–18 War. She would never say anything directly to anyone's discredit but she had, I felt, strong reservations about some people and some of the ways of the world in general. After recounting some incident which did not show the participants up in a particularly good light, she would sigh sadly and say something like 'It takes all sorts to make a world' or 'Of course, everyone is entitled to their own point of view' making it abundantly clear that it was something of which she would have no part.

She did not, however, always take refuge in platitudes. I remember her once saying, apropos nothing in particular: 'Never tell a lie to save yourself but it is sometimes right to tell a lie to save someone else.'

I think she probably had something of the stuff of which martyrs are made. At the same time I am sure that she knew far more of the world's wicked ways than her rather prim, virginal appearance might suggest.

If I had thought much about being grown-up at that time then I would have thought of it in the context of a woman's world. After all the whole of my upbringing had been in the hands of women with my father as a remote figure with whose way of life it was almost impossible to identify. It was Nurse Webster who first inspired me to imagine myself as the macho male, the righter of wrongs and the champion of the oppressed. At night I would fall asleep dreaming of myself telling a lie to save Nurse Webster's honour or other ways of saving her from a fate worse than death.

Sadly, in the middle of my first term at Alton Burn, Mum wrote to say that Nurse Webster was very ill and would like a letter from me. Letters of sympathy are hard enough to write when one is grown up. For a six-year-old, going on seven it was a formidable task indeed. I wrestled with it for days. I even thought of splashing tears on the paper to demonstrate the depth of my feelings. In the end my letter arrived the day she died and her sister wrote to say it had been put in her coffin.

CHAPTER FIVE

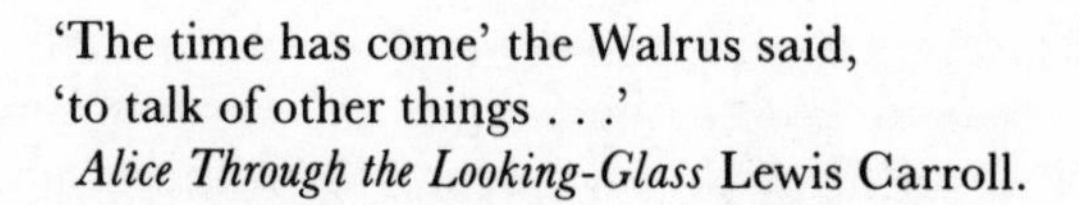

'The time has come' the Walrus said,
'to talk of other things . . .'
Alice Through the Looking-Glass Lewis Carroll.

The school holidays that spring were marked by an event which might in itself have been of little importance but which had remarkable consequences for both Gordon and me. It came upon us quite unexpectedly.

One day, early in the holidays it was announced that we were to accompany our parents on another trip into Aberdeen. Such expeditions were not always welcomed by us unless there was some particular object in view. For the most part we would far rather spend our time mucking about on the farm or attending to our growing interests which now included some chickens of our own and an adoptive calf each. By comparison trips to a town were often incredibly boring. The normal form was, after the car had been garaged, for a headquarters to be established in the Palace Hotel in Union Street*, and for us to be sent off to do our own thing, armed with a sixpence each or, on red letter days, a shilling, with orders to re-assemble in time for lunch at some stated time. We would invariably make our way down to the docks to gaze at the cargo boats and liners from all over the world and wonder at the appearance of the ships' crews of every nationality on earth hanging around the street corners. Sometimes, as an extra thrill there would be one of the boats from Orkney or Shetland docked in its berth which we would look upon with considerable nostalgia.

* Burnt down just after the last war.

One of the greatest irritations of the day would be when we got back to the Palace Hotel at the appointed hour, eager to get started on the invariably highly satisfactory lunch which the hotel provided, only to find our parents having a fine time with some of their friends in the lounge – cocktail bars had not yet 'arrived' in Aberdeen – and with obviously little intention of getting down to the real business of the table for quite some time. There can be nothing more tedious for a starving child than to be set down with a glass of orange squash and a straw and told to be seen and not heard until the grown-ups are good and ready. Even in the plush surroundings of a luxury hotel, however, there was the occasional opportunity for adventure.

I can remember one particularly exciting happening. We had excused ourselves, Gordon and I, on the pretext that we required to go to the lavatory. The facilities at the Palace Hotel were, to our unsophisticated eyes, in very truth palatial. It was an extravagance of marble floors, great mirrors and serried ranks of wash-hand basins with gleaming taps and exotic bottles of various pomades. But most intriguing of all was the row of polished mahogany booths which lined the whole of one wall to which gentleman could gain access on the payment of one penny inserted in a slot in order to complete their toilet.

On this particular day Gordon and I, greatly daring, paid our one penny tribute and jointly set about exploring the inside of one of these boxes. The first thing which we discovered was that someone, by use of a nail file or other sharp instrument, had scratched a short poem on the exquisitely polished woodwork which read in its entirety: Here lies a Scotsman,/ Broken hearted./ He paid a penny/ And only farted!

This simple poetic offering threw us into such paroxysms of mirth that we had to hold each other up whilst our sides rocked. We stamped the floor with glee and tears ran down our faces. Then one of us spotted a Swan Vestas match-box lying at the back of the lavatory seat. On examining this more closely we found it to be packed tightly with what appeared to be pound notes. That sobered us down quite speedily. What was to be done? Our first instinct was to purloin the box and say nothing.

Then it occurred to us that that would be stealing and, if we were found out, we might easily spend the rest of our lives in prison. And, come to that, what could we do with a whole lot of neatly folded pound notes? We had nowhere to spend them and nothing to spend them on. In the end we placed the box exactly where we had found it and, bolting out of the cubicle, sped upstairs to report our discovery to higher authority. They took a bit of convincing of our excited burblings but, in the end, Dad agreed to come with us to see what it was all about. When we opened the door again the match-box had vanished without a trace. A protracted search and the spending of more pennies contributed nothing to finding a solution. It has remained with me all these years as one of the great unexplained mysteries of my life.

It can be imagined that, over lunch, there was a great deal of hilarity at our expense whilst we protested over and over again of the reality of the match-box, to no avail whatever.

This was the day on which Dad, with no relevance to anything else, suddenly announced that he was going to take us shopping. He was a non-drinker for medical reasons and he had probably got bored as the port continued to circulate. Anyway off we set and we finished up to our great surprise in Martin's fishing tackle shop. Dad himself was not a fisherman but he had suddenly got it into his head that fishing was something we should do. There were long and serious consultations as a result of which sometime later we emerged each the proud possessor of a nine-foot Greenheart trout rod, a reel and line and a variety of sizes of worm hooks on gut. For good measure he also bought each of us a knife, not of the conventional sort with a gadget for taking nails out of horses' hooves but one for taking hooks out of fishes mouths. And that was the event which I mentioned at the beginning of this chapter which was to be the beginning of a lifetime's passion for both of us. I noted however that Dad blenched visibly when it came to paying for it all. There was practically no change out of a ten pound note.

I do not suppose that Dad, when he bought us our fishing rods had given a great deal of thought to the subject of where we might go fishing but such matters in those days were not of great importance, particularly if one's ambitions rose no higher than trying one's luck with a worm in a burn. Apart from the great salmon rivers such as the Dee, the Don and the Deveron for which Aberdeenshire is now world-famous, there were many smaller streams where trout abounded. But in a still more modest category there was a legion of rushy little burns where the water sparkled and tumbled, most of them no wider than you could jump across with ease. I say 'were' in the past tense but of course they are still there. It is only that modern farming methods and the use of pesticides and artificial manures has sterilised the countryside to a degree which has destroyed most forms of wild life and with it the lively little brown trout which abounded in the streams.

It is also the law in Scotland that fishing for brown trout has never been regarded as an offence. Indeed in more spacious days it was the law that it was no offence to take salmon. The salmon which swarmed up Scotland's rivers were regarded as the rightful food of the people as much as the deer in the hills. The only rigorous law pertaining to the migrating salmon was against killing them in the strictly-defined spawning season. A second conviction for this crime according to a 1426 Act of Parliament was punishable by death as an offence against the property of the people. Perhaps it might not be such a bad idea to re-introduce this legislation to combat the poaching gangs of modern times with their lethal monfil nets which they trawl off the estuaries and, more particularly, the inland gangs who use cyanide to destroy all life indiscriminately in our rivers. But I am now back to sixty years ago when God was in his heaven and all was still right with the world.

Let it not be thought that to catch a trout with a worm was merely a matter of dangling a worm under its nose at the end of a stick, a bit of string and a bent pin. Jocky and his younger brother Billy had their own method of catching trout. This was by a method known as 'guddling' and involved lying flat on your tummy on the river bank, gently putting one hand in the water and cautiously feeling your way until you touched the under-belly of the fish which was lying unsuspectingly under the overhang of the bank. The fish, so it is claimed, finds this gentle touch of the fingers so agreeable that it allows you to feel your way caressingly up its body. When the head is reached, you make a sudden grab, inserting your predatory fingers into the creature's open gills and so lifting it out of the water. Many a time I have heard respectable Captains of Industry boasting to me nostalgically of the guddling exploits of their youth. Frankly I don't believe a word of it. I only once saw Jocky catch a fish in this way and I think he was very lucky at that. Maybe a poacher on a dark night might take a big salmon lying under a boulder by this method and he deserves his prize. It is not a profitable occupation for the amateur, however enthusiastic.

At the same time a fishing rod such as I had just acquired was not, in the normal course of events, something that Jocky or Billy would have been able to lay their hands on.

'Ma Gawd! Thon's a wonner!' as Jocky said when he first laid eyes on it. I am not quite sure whether by 'wonner' he meant a 'wonder' or a 'winner'. I rather think the latter. Either would have been right in my view.

There is the consideration that before you set out to lure a trout to a hook baited with a worm that you must first catch your worm. Nor is it a case of any old worm doing just as well as the next. The big, pale red-blue worms that you might turn over when digging in the garden or find under a flat stone are not a great deal of good. What is needed is the small, bright-red banded worm, called a brandling, which has its natural habitat in a cow pat or, more conveniently, in a midden.

In those days the whole life of a farm like Tullochford revolved round the midden. It occupied the centre of the farm steading with the byre along the top side, the mill and storehouses along one side with the pig houses opposite and the stables and cart-shed down at the bottom. Twice a day, at the mucking out of the byres, barrow loads of manure were run out over it on planks to be tipped and, with the pig house and the stables contributing their daily quotas, a giant compost heap was built up over the year against the coming of spring when it would be carted out to fertilise the fields. A minor role for the midden was to provide brandlings for our fishing expeditions which were soon to become daily adventures.

Our favourite burn was about half a mile over the fields. On the very first day, having carefully baited my hook, I dropped it rather tentatively into the water to be rewarded instantly with a sharp tug on my line. I tugged back smartly and a moment later my first trout was dancing merrily on the grass. I suppose it was at that moment that a lifelong addiction to fishing was born in me. That afternoon we caught ten little trout – fortunately, for the maintainance of peace between us, exactly five each – and we had them for breakfast the following morning, split open and cooked in melted butter.

That was the spring when Dad had the milking machine installed and the dairy farming started to move into top gear. It was driven by a motor which was in itself a great innovation although all the lighting was still by paraffin lamps slung from the rafters and water for the milk cooler was pumped by the windmill, as was all the water for the house and cottages.

The windmill was a tall gaunt skeletal construction, made of galvanised iron which stood out in the stack yard. Whilst it whirled merrily away for most of the time, there were occasions when a drop in the wind, lasting more than a day or two, would cause great anxiety. Milk in those days was not the sterilised product we know today. Coming straight from the cow, it was merely water-cooled before being put into ten gallon cans to be put at our road-end from where it was picked up by a milk lorry and driven into Aberdeen to the milk co-operative. Milk which had not been properly cooled could not be sent away and simply had to be poured down the drain but as children we never drank cooled milk. It was brought into the house warm from the cow.

The visit of the milk recorder once a month was something to be looked forward to with mixed feelings. The milk recorder was usually a lady. She arrived with all her bottles and testing equipment and stayed overnight. Her function was to carry out tests for tuberculosis and to monitor the butter fat content of the milk. It was, of course, very bad news indeed if any of the herd was found to be tubercular. Infection could usually be traced to dirt and any suspicion of dirt about a dairy farm was a very serious matter indeed. Despite every precaution a tubercular cow was sometimes detected which led to a tremendous cleanliness campaign and particularly on the personal cleanliness of anyone handling the milk. A speck of dirt flicked into a two-gallon pail of milk being carried from the byre to the dairy where it was cooled could contaminate a whole ten-gallon can.

The milk recorder's tests also showed the quality of the milk given by each cow in terms of butter fat. The butter fat content of milk varies greatly from breed to breed as well as between individual animals in a herd. By and large pure Friesian cattle have the lowest percentage of butter fat whilst in breeds such as Jerseys and Guernseys it is very high. Friesians, on the other hand, generally have a higher milk yield. Thus it is the old question of quality or quantity. Our herd was largely made up of a Friesian-Ayrshire cross which basically made for the best of both worlds. At the same time the butter fat content of each cow's milk varied as much as from 2·5 percent to 4 percent and over. A Jersey, on the other hand would give milk of around 6 percent. There was another statistic which was the subject of absorbing interest to everyone on the farm and this was each cow's milk yield. Rather like cricketing addicts who keep the most precise records of performances with bat and ball and where the first batsman to reach a thousand runs in a season is a great milestone, so it was for us when a cow produced a thousand gallons. This would mean a cow producing around five gallons a day over ten months of the year which represents a formidable performance by any standards. After the milk recorder's monthly visit the records were carefully scrutinised and there was great satisfaction all round if the showing was a good one.

Although Tullochford was in some of the most fertile and

intensively farmed land in a county as famed for its productivity as Aberdeenshire, it was, by the standards of today, remote. It stood almost exactly in the middle of a triangle with the villages of Old Meldrum, Tarves and Fyvie each almost exactly five miles distant and, with larger farms spaced out about a mile apart, there was no corporate life such as you would find centered round the average English country village where the honest sons of the soil were wont to forgather after a day of toil to partake of a convivial pint of ale or two. Pubs in Scotland were, and by and large still are, for town dwellers and, sixty years ago were uncompromisingly sawdust-on-the-floor places where men went for the serious business of drinking and it was pretty well unheard of for women to show a leg.

Thus each farm was perforce a self-contained community of around fifteen souls who lived day by day and every day in each others' pockets. There was in consequence a family spirit and a pride in the achievement of the family. There was also a competitiveness with other farms which was, if anything, keener than might exist between rival football teams. At such events as ploughing matches or local horse shows this rivalry would reach fever pitch.

Nowhere was this pride and rivalry more in evidence than when the horses were being prepared for a show. Every bit of their harness was polished to a standard which would have done credit to the turnout of the Household Cavalry at the changing of the guard at Buckingham Palace. Every bit of metal was burnished until it shone like silver and the decorative horse brasses, now so sought after by collectors of such bygone relics, displayed with all the panache of a knight of old riding into battle. On the eve of a horse show a horseman would sit up far into the night braiding his horse's mane and tail with the most skilfully contrived adornments and combing the silky hair of its fetlocks as if it was the crowning glory of a Hollywood film star. I can still vividly recall the smell of exotic unguents and polishes which pervaded the stables in the days preceding an important show. The reward was simply a certificate, or perhaps a rosette, nailed to the beam above the horse's stall. It was enough.

At the height of that summer, when the corn was ripening under a sun riding high in the clear blue sky, there came the bad news. N.G. wrote in a letter which accompanied Gordon's usual devastatingly awful report, that he felt it might be better if I joined the school for the autumn term instead of waiting until the spring as had been intended.

Thus it came about that at the age of six, three months before my seventh birthday, I was to be launched into the world of which I had been so long in dread. Often at night I would wake up sweating with fear from a nightmare in which the figure of N.G. would assume proportions far more terrifying than anything inspired by Dracula. Now the moment of truth was just round the corner.

There was, however, an unexpected bonus before term took up in the middle of September. It had been a long hot summer with the result that the harvest came earlier than usual. Harvests seem to come much earlier these days and nor (or is it my imagination?) are they nearly so much dependent on the weather. In those days there was much anxious scanning of the skies as the climax of the whole farming year drew near. A sudden spell of rainy weather and great tracts of the crop would be battered to lie flat and green and only capable of being harvested by being scythed by hand. The better the crop, the heavier the heads of grain, the worse the disaster. On the other hand who wanted a light crop with short straw? The straw, now ignored by the giant mechanical harvesters which gobble up the crop in great swathes was an important part of the harvest and required to provide bedding for the cattle for the rest of the year.

That year the weather was such that the harvest started right at the beginning of September. The preparations were almost as exciting as the harvest itself. The binder had to be dragged out of the implement shed where it had lain neglected since being put away the previous year. Meantime birds would have nested in it and it would have settled under a mantle of dust so that it was with considerable anxiety that it was checked over to ensure that it was still in good working order. Then there was the distaff side of the operation. A huge cask of beer would have arrived which had to be installed in the big larder, set up on blocks and allowed to settle. There was much baking of bread to be done, tea urns to be given their annual outing and extra stores to be ordered from the grocer in Old Meldrum.

On the first day of the harvest it was a case of all available male labour on parade which included us and several of the neighbouring crofters who would eventually get their own corn strips cut in return. Once the cutting of a field had been started the harvesters were out there all day until sundown whilst the women organised a regular supply column to the front line of battle – stretchers loaded with mounds of bread, whole cheeses and pounds of butter, pickled onions and all the rest. There would be gallons of tea brought out in hay-boxes and which needed constant replenishing and beer in two-gallon milk pails which seemed to need refilling even more often. There was a feeling of festivity in the air and all that was lacking were the swings and roundabouts.

The horse-drawn binder was an extremely ingenious piece of machinery even if it did have a distinct 'Heath Robinson' air about it. It was fitted with 'sails' which whirled round to push the standing corn against the cutting blades of the mower. The cut corn was then carried on a canvas conveyor sheet which delivered it to the binding machine which tied it into sheaves with binder twine and which were then tossed out to be collected by the stookers following the binder who set them up in stooks, generally in sets of six sheaves.

There were, of course, a great number of things which could go wrong in the production line and, in fact, very often did. On an average the binder would have to be halted every couple of hours or so to remedy one fault or another. The most usual was that the binding machine was not tying the knots properly or the supply of binder twine had become exhausted with the result that the sheaves could not be set up in their stooks and the whole operation would have to be halted.

The job of the stooker was not an easy one and particularly for a small boy in short trousers and with bare arms. One of the menaces was that every now and again the binder would hit a patch of thistles in the standing corn with the result that the end product would be a bundle more prickly than any hedgehog. There is no thistle more prickly than the Scotch variety which is part of the insignia of the country and bears the warning in Latin *nemo me impune lacessit* – 'Nobody touches me without getting hurt'. You can, as they say, say that again!

Then, too, from time to time the binder would throw out the odd sheaf untied. This the stooker had to take in his stride, quickly improvising a truss of straw to hold the sheaf together without, as it were, breaking step. Whenever we, or any other of the farm youngsters, took our place with the stooking team we were not given any allowance on account of our size. We had to keep up the pace. It involved grabbing two sheaves, one tucked under each arm, carrying them to the site for the next stook, setting them exactly in line with the previous stook and at exactly the same distance apart and putting them together with the two sheaves carried by your partner so that they propped each other up firmly. A badly set up pair of sheaves would cause the whole stook to collapse. To look back down the line of stooks and find that one of them had subsided was an extremely shaming experience.

The method of cutting a field was for the binder to cut the first swathe round the outside of the four sides of the field and then continue round and round as the patch of standing corn grew ever smaller and the sides shorter. It was however a long business and the harvesting of, say, a twenty-acre field might take up to three days. Whilst all through the long day the harvesters existed largely with pit stops to take on a mug of tea or down a pint of beer, there were regular breaks called when everyone would take a rest, gnaw away at their mammoth sandwiches and indulge in light, and often ribald, banter. The great comradeship of the harvest field is well illustrated by an incident which I remember from those far-off days.

It happened that Jimmy Pratt, the grieve, had acquired a brand new set of false teeth which was his great pride and the envy of all. During one of the breaks that day Tommy Rendall, the head cattleman was wrestling with a particularly tough crust which was proving too much for his gumless jaws.

'Ach, Jimmy' he said eventually 'gie's a loan of yer teeth 'til I get this crust champit.' Without a word Jimmy handed his teeth over. Tommy then, having 'champit awa' on his crust to his satisfaction, handed them back with a cursory nod of thanks.

And so the golden days sped by.

The morning came when, dressed in my blue school blazer, with red piping round the lapels and cuffs and with the trunk containing all my sartorial needs for the next three months loaded into the back of the Austin, we set off for Inverurie Railway Station; next stop Alton Burn, Preparatory School for Young Gentlemen, by Nairn and looking out over the bleak waters of the Moray Firth.

CHAPTER SIX

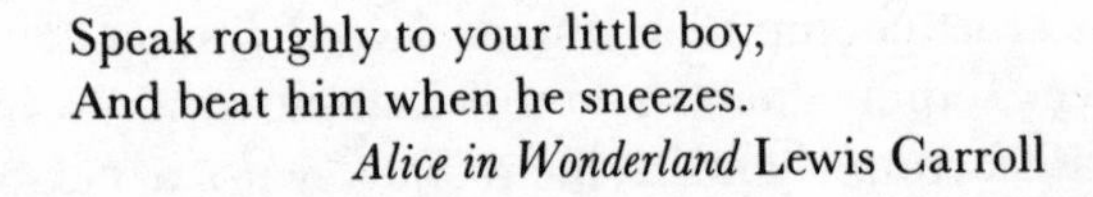

Speak roughly to your little boy,
And beat him when he sneezes.
Alice in Wonderland Lewis Carroll

Inverurie Station when we arrived there presented a scene of considerable animation. There were at least half a dozen boys who, with their distinctive red and blue blazers and school caps were evidently bound for the same destination. In those days all travellers on the railways were divided into three carefully delineated financial – or was it social? – categories, marked in large numbers painted on the carriage, first, second or third Class. A small army of porters scurried to and fro, loading our big school trunks and trundling them off on barrows to be loaded into the guard's van whilst we scrambled into the first class carriage where seats had been reserved for us, presumably by the school. Then came that dreaded and seemingly interminable wait whilst we hung out of the windows, gazing down miserably at our assorted parents shuffling about on the platform below us, desperately trying to think of some last minute messages of encouragement or good cheer and failing dreadfully. The relief all round when the Station Master finally blew his whistle and the train started to steam out of the station was tangible. We frantically waved our still-white handkerchiefs out of the windows at the rapidly-diminishing figures waving back from the platform until a bend in the line finally and mercifully obscured them from view. Then we assembled back in our railway carriage and the time had come to take stock.

There were six of us in all, including Gordon and me, seated silently three a side, gazing at one another. One of them, the elder of two Gordon brothers, was, like brother Gordon, an old hand beginning his second year. His younger brother Harry, a new boy like myself, was a rather sickly looking lad who suffered from adenoids and had a bent arm which was, I later learned, as a result of it being badly set after he had broken it when he was younger. From their initials H.A.G. and L.A.G. they were inevitably known for the rest of their school days as 'Hag' and 'Lag'. Almost every boy at school acquired a nickname, usually of a rather derogatory nature. I was much alarmed to learn that my brother had acquired the soubriquet of 'Slops' and thus I was immediately to become known to all as 'Slops Two' to my great irritation and annoyance. The fifth occupant of our carriage was a very large boy whose short trousers already were showing signs of becoming too tight for him and of developing into a regular Billy Bunter, called 'Doffy' Forbes and finally there was Jock Crawford, a freckled, fair-haired boy with a wide, infectious grin who was soon to become my very best friend.

The silence which had descended on us after the temporary loss of our various parents, was not to last for very long. What with one thing leading to another, a push here and a shove there, we were soon ragging away in fine style. By the time the train pulled into Nairn we were six rather dishevelled looking little boys and all the very best of friends. Suddenly, such is the resilience of youth, the harvest field at Tullochford seemed very far away indeed.

Alton Burn was a tiny school, mustering only about twenty boys at full strength, thus the four new boys on the train represented almost the whole of the autumn term intake. There were, in fact, two more and as new boys the six of us were to share a small dormitory of our own. The other two were a boy called Rodney Hitchcock, not a very Scottish name but whose father was the owner of a well-known fishing hotel at Lochmaddy on the island of North Uist in the Outer Hebrides and Geordie Dudgeon whose father was a very big sheep farmer at Loth, on the coast of Sutherland, beyond Brora.

There were only two classrooms and only two dormitories and the way the system worked was this. The new intake and the intake for the previous year shared one classroom with the senior boys in the front row of desks and the new boys in the row behind. The rest of the school shared the big classroom and all three of the senior years, the big dormitory. As I think I have already remarked, a schoolboy's life, from the tenderest age, is governed by seniority of years. Even a matter of a few months is sufficient to establish a place nearer the sun.

I can still remember the most senior boys at Alton Burn when I arrived; boys with all the authority that years calculated in double figures can bring. There was 'Noony' Lauder whose father had been knighted for services to the Empire but, much more importantly, had once played rugger for Scotland. There was 'Bunny' Lahore whose father was also a knight and Governor of an Indian Province which meant that Bunny had to spend his school holidays with an aunt in Arbroath. Finally there was 'Swotty' Lilburn and 'Tiger' Kynoch-Shand who made up the quorum of School Prefects who had the power to administer corporal punishment (gym slipper only) to those of their juniors found guilty of the more venial offences. These demi-gods of eleven or twelve years conducted themselves with an assurance and sophistication which could not but command admiration verging on hero-worship.

The basis of any form of institutional living must depend on the laying down of strictly enforceable rules by which all the inmates must abide or else risk dire retribution. Anything less must lead to anarchy. This at least was the philosophy which was held to sixty years ago and which, it was generally conceded, had contributed in greatest measure to the building of the British Empire and the successes which over the centuries had attended our armed forces in the furthest flung corners of the world. It was the tradition on which all our boarding schools had been founded and indeed the thole-pin of family life in all properly conducted households. 'Spare the rod and spoil the child' was a truth which no sensible person would consider worth argument and of which the fact that the Battle of Waterloo was said to have been won on the playing fields of Eton College was a living testimony. There was no more enthusiastic upholder of this truth than Major N.G. Pearson M.C., late of The Gordon Highlanders, headmaster and sole proprietor of Alton Burn.

The routine into which we were plunged with effect from the first morning after our arrival started ominously. We lived by a series of bells and gongs. First bell went at seven thirty in the morning when one was required to shed one's pyjamas, tie a towel round one's waist and join the queue of shivering fellow pupils for a plunge into a cold bath. This was supervised by Matron who sat, implacable and unmoving, on a wooden chair at the tap end of the single bath ('wallow' in the school vernacular) which served the whole school. Matron was an extremely large, but not altogether unprepossessing, lady who bulged in her blue-striped uniform in ample folds, both above and below her four-inch-wide starched white belt. It was in fact only a quick swish in and out again and was said to set the blood flowing properly for the rest of the day.

The single bath with which the school was equipped might have presented problems when it came to more conventional bathing but this was something which was easily overcome by efficient organisation. Each boy had one bath night a week, which he had in common with four other boys, from Monday to Friday. Saturdays were reserved for communal mud-scraping after games and Sunday was not a day when it was proper to indulge in such a Sybaritic activity according to the strict observances of the Presbyterian Kirk.

Morning service was at eight o'clock. This was conducted by N.G. in person and largely confined to the singing of the *Te Deum* and the *Magnificat* to both of which N.G. was greatly addicted and accompanied by Mrs Pearson on the piano.

Breakfast was invariably porridge, with bread and butter, although jam was permitted if a second slice of bread was indulged in. A novelty at breakfast for me was tea. At the farm we were only ever given milk to drink and to begin with I could not stand the taste of tea. This was something I was, perforce, soon to get over.

Lessons began at nine o'clock and there were three 'periods' before lunch. Every afternoon was devoted to games, with boxing or gymnastics in the gymnasium if weather conditions were considered too bad for outdoors but this was a rare occurrence.

Then there was tea and, afterwards, one more lesson period, followed by an hour of prep. After that we had a cup of cocoa and another slice of bread and butter before bed and lights out at eight.

I have forgotten one little ceremony round which the whole of our day, after a fashion, revolved. This took place at two o'clock exactly each afternoon. Every boy was permitted to bring back to school a tin of sweets, large enough to last him the whole term and from which he was allowed to select three sweets a day. It was for this purpose that the two o'clock sweet parade took place after lunch each day. The tins were stored in a large locked cupboard in the small classroom. Most boys brought one of those large tins of assorted hard and soft centres and this created a recurring agonising crisis of decision making. Two hard centres and one soft? Or vice versa? A vanilla or a rose cream? Needless to say it was not something that one was allowed to linger over if only for the press of eager boys behind in the queue awaiting their turn in a fever of anticipation.

The daily rationing of sweets, however, had another important role to play in our lives. It was an integral part of the disciplinary code. One of the penalties for one of the more minor breaches of the rules was to have one's sweet ration cut or even withdrawn altogether for a certain number of days. This penalty could be imposed for an offence as minor as not leaving one's bedroom slippers tidily under the bed to more serious things like whistling or putting one's hands in one's trouser pockets.

I suppose, judged in the light of the more indulgent attitude today towards child delinquency, this may seem to have been rather petty and even far-fetched but it was enforced with a rigour which must now seem positively Dickensian. There occurred in my second term at Alton Burn an incident in this connection which, in retrospect, must seem to put N.G. somewhere to the right of Wackford Squeers of Dotheboys Hall as a disciplinarian of the first rank. It happened that one boy took pity on another temporarily deprived of his sweet ration and, in a show of immense generosity, gave him a small broken chip from one of his humbugs. It was whilst the recipient of this unexpected windfall was crunching it with the greatest show of satisfaction that the movement of his jaws was spotted by N.G. He went suddenly puce in the face and demanded to know of the boy the name of his benefactor. He then retired to his study to spend the rest of the day considering what might be a suitable punishment for an offence of such enormity.

The answer came about half an hour after lights out. Then the bell sounded and everybody was ordered downstairs to the main classroom in their pyjamas where they were required to witness the administration of six stokes of the cane on the bare bottoms of the two offenders.

It should be said that this was an abnormal departure from the system of crime and punishment which prevailed. This was based on a points system which in a way was even more sadistic.

The way it worked was this. There was a chart put up on the school notice board which listed the names of all the boys in the school down the left-hand side and along the top ran the dates from the first day of term to the last. Opposite each boy's name were two lines on which were recorded in red, on the top line, what were described as 'Mullets' and, below this what were described as 'Bars' which were in blue. In more simple terms they should be described as Stars and Stripes. A star was a good mark and a stripe was a bad mark. To have earned good mark was acknowledged by a red dot opposite after the name of the boy to whom it had been awarded. To have earned a bad mark was to have a similar dot recorded on the line below in blue. To have four dots accumulated after your name was to earn a full Mullet or, more significantly a full Bar. To have a full Mullet set against your name was shown thus, in red: Sutherland $^{*}_{*}X^{*}_{*}$

Or, with four bad marks, the equivalent in blue. Anyone who accumulated four full Bars got beaten but an accumulation of Mullets did not win any material reward, like an extra sweet ration or something. They were however set against any bad marks so that a regular Mullet earner was unlikely ever to be in peril. My brother Gordon was a compulsive earner of Bars and got beaten on average about once a fortnight whilst I, from the very start of my school career, was always safely in the red.

This chart was like a league table. N.G. filled it out each night so that everyone's first action in the morning was to rush down to discover what good or bad marks they had earned the previous day. They could be awarded for anything to do with lessons, a good or bad prep or by a recommendation from one of the other teachers for something in daily lessons. Thus every boy in the school not only followed his own progress or regress but that of every other boy in the school with the same absorbed interest and attention as is given, in real life, to the position of one's favourite football team or pop group in the charts.

Whilst N.G. ran his ship with all the ruthless efficiency of a Captain Bligh whose word was the whole law, he had under-officers to help him as teaching staff. Chief amongst these was Mr MacCarthy, who taught mathematics and history, but there was also Miss Brydon, a tall spinsterish lady with her hair done up in a high bun. She was always dressed in varying shades of brown and invariably pulled galoshes over her elastic-sided boots whenever she went out and regardless of the weather. Miss Brydon's main teaching subject was geography and it was rumoured that when she retired she was planning to take a trip up the Amazon. Finally there was Miss Stewart, known to all the boys as 'Stewbug'. Her job was to coach any of the younger boys who were backward in reading or writing. 'Stewbug' was desperately and painfully in love with Mr MacCarthy and always blushed a bright pink even when she passed him in a corridor.

Officially no boy was supposed to come to the school unless

he could already read and do proper joined-up writing as well as simple mathematics. However some were more backward than others and such, I suspect, was the narrow margin of profitability that N.G. could not really afford to pass up the prospect of a new pupil simply on the grounds that he did not come up to the educational standard he himself had laid down. It was Stewbug's main job to see that they caught up but she also understudied Mr MacCarthy or Miss Brydon whenever required.

N.G. himself, whom nobody was allowed to understudy – nor indeed would they have been capable of doing – taught Latin and Scripture. For more senior boys he gave lessons on the tactics of the 1914–1918 War which included instruction on how to construct proper trenches with a parapet, a parados, underground command dug-outs and a decent system of communication trenches. This was in anticipation of the next war which he was convinced was not very far off and for which he saw it as his duty to prepare his pupils to play their part.

If I have given the impression that the regime at Alton Burn was a harsh one and the shock to the system of a delicately-nurtured boy such as myself equivalent to the first shock of that regular early morning cold bath, then the impression I have given is the correct one. The regime was pretty well par for the course for any private boarding school in those days and indeed N.G.'s regime may well have been more benign than some. It was unthinkable that any boy from a certain class of society, at a time when the social classes were far more sharply defined than they are today, should have any other sort of education; and that was that. For the victims themselves to feel any resentment against the system simply did not occur. There might have been a stifled sob or two after lights-out in the dorm on the first night of term but protracted bouts of home-sickness were unusual. The requirements of survival were far too urgent.

A far greater hazard than to fall foul of the laid-down disciplinary rules was the bullying by other boys. The school rules may have been harsh but by and large they were administered impartially. The persecution of one boy by another boy or, as was often the case, by a group of boys was another matter altogether. It is in the nature of some boys to be bullies and the fate of others to be among the bullied. It is the bullying which is apt to scar a boy for life. The Harry Flashmans of *Tom Brown's Schooldays* have always been far more real than fictional.

I can remember my first few days at Alton Burn very clearly indeed although it is now over sixty-five years ago. After all to be chucked in at the deep end, as must happen to everyone at various stages of a full life, is apt to be a memorable experience. I can also remember the build-up to the last day of term equally vividly.

There was a sort of litany which we started to sing as the day of our final release drew near. I think the verses were in fact common to most schools, having spread from one to another in some mysterious way. It went:

No more beetles in my tea
Making googlie eyes at me.
No more tadpoles in my bath,
Trying hard to make me laugh.

And so on, with lots more 'no mores'. Our version finished up.

In (. . .) days, we'll be free,
Out of the hands of N.G.P.

The song was sung with great gusto as the days slipped by. Some boys improvised calendars which they kept in their desks and ticked off the days one by one, rather like it is said prisoners do on the walls of their cells.

N.G. and Lucy Pearson joined into the spirit of things with the greatest of enthusiasm, probably more relieved than any of us that the end of yet another term was in sight. Traditionally at the end of each term, they laid on a great feast for all the boys, called the 'Guzz' – presumably short for guzzle. This was preceeded by a party in the main classroom when we all sang carols. Although we had all the traditional Christmas carols like 'The Holly and the Ivy' and 'Good King Wenceslaus' the highlights were a sort of syncopated effort in which N.G. sang the first two lines in the original Latin in basso-very-profondo with Lucy thundering on the piano in support; then we would all repeat the two lines in English in our high treble voices. Thus, N.G.:

Caput apri deferro,
Ferens laudes Domino:

Then all of us:

The boar's head in hand I bear,
Singing praises to the Lord . . .

and so on through many verses. It was all very inspiriting.

Then to the Guzz itself. Like everything else that N.G. organised, timing was of the essence. First of all lots were drawn. The boys drawing low numbers were the lucky ones, putting them at the head of the queue. This was formed in the corridor leading to the dining hall where we all lined up, chittering with excitement, to wait for the gong to sound. Then, exactly to the second of seven o'clock, at the first thump of the gong, we raced, cheering wildly, down the corridor each trying to elbow his way to the front and then scrambled to find chairs as near as possible to one or other of the teachers seated at the end of each of the long tables, with the proudest seats of all on either side of N.G. himself, all the trials and tribulations of the term forgotten.

As to the rest of my first term, the bit in between the beginning and the end, I do not now remember a great deal except for the friends I made. At my desk which was second from the end of the back row of the small classroom, I had

Jock Crawford on one side and Rodney Hitchcock on the other, with 'Bratter' Gordon one desk further away. The four of us, put together by the merest chance, became firm friends, perhaps as much in self defence as new boys as anything else, but they were friendships which were to last for the rest of our lives.

CHAPTER SEVEN

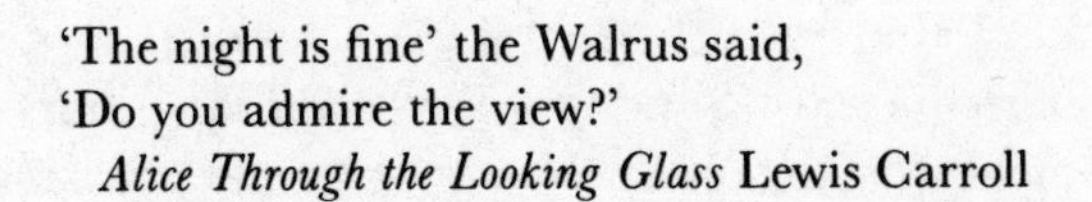

> 'The night is fine' the Walrus said,
> 'Do you admire the view?'
> *Alice Through the Looking Glass* Lewis Carroll

It was on my first Christmas holidays back from school, my seventh Christmas on earth, that I became precociously aware that I was developing a split personality. I don't mean a split personality in the mould of Dr Jekyll and Mr Hyde but more of a feeling of being two people. It was a case of remaining the same inside but looking out on two totally different worlds. One was the world of Alton Burn, ruled by the formidable figure of N.G. and with people like Jock and Harry and 'Doffy' Forbes or 'Tiger' Kynoch-Shand or 'Bunny' Lahore all struggling over such abstruse matters as the declension of Latin verbs or trying to remember the name of the capital of Mexico with intervals of chasing an oval ball up and down a muddy field. The other was life at Tullochford with friends like Jocky and Billy Pratt and Nurse Webster and where life revolved round getting the daily quota of milk cans off every morning or excitements such as whether the cow which had been lowing all night had had a bull or a heifer calf.

It was, in fact, just the same as the grown-up world of our parents but in minature. Their life was also lived in two completely different worlds between which there was simply no form of communication. One world was the farming world. Dad took his farming very seriously and, in this world, they numbered amongst their close friends some of the most prominent farmers in the county. Our nearest neighbour who had Crichie Farm about three miles away was John Strachan who was not only one of the most astute of men when it came to anything to do with agriculture in general and breeding Aberdeen Angus in particular – 'lang-heided' was the Scottish description which most aptly described him – but was also well-known throughout Aberdeenshire and beyond for a popular weekly programme he had on the radio. He conducted this in the broadest Aberdeenshire dialect which is one of the most distinctive and expressive of the many variations of the Scottish accent. We would all go over to lunch at Crichie most Sundays. This Sunday 'dinner', as the midday meal was always known, was a great occasion for us. The Strachans had three sons and a daughter so there were ten of us who sat down to table with Mr Strachan, the benign and slightly-perspiring dispenser of hospitality, seated at the head. And what hospitality! If the board did not actually groan under the weight of the immense side of beef set in front of him, it was only because it was made of the stoutest oak, fit for a mediaeval wassail.

Another near neighbour was Leslie Durno of Upper Mill Farm. The Durnos were one of the great farming dynasties of Aberdeenshire who owned between them some of the best-known farming land in the county. Leslie was accounted the foremost judge of Shorthorn cattle in Scotland whilst his brother Jim, over on the other side of Inverurie, was a revered figure in Aberdeen Angus circles. Then there was Mr Argo of Petty, whose large ears stuck out from his head and were almost completely transparent, like a bat's. He was a prominent breeder of Clydesdales and a widower, whose teenage daughter, Peggy, kept house for him and for whom my brother Gordon conceived one of his earliest adolescent passions.

Although at this time the 1920s were moving into the 1930s and the onset of the great agricultural depression which was to match the industrial depression of the inter-war years and see the tragedy of hunger marches, it was difficult to imagine any life more comfortably secure than that of the Strachans, the Durnos and their fellows. Nor would I, and even more Gordon, have ever dreamed of looking beyond the horizons of a world where we were so content.

There was however the other side of our parents' lives which started, at this time, to intrude more and more on our own. It was, I suppose, an inevitable spin-off from our other existence at Alton Burn. Jock Crawford's parents lived only a dozen miles away, near neighbours in the eyes of country-dwellers, whilst 'Hag' and 'Lag' Gordon were only sightly further away at the other side of Old Meldrum. Both families were great buddies with Mum and Dad and were always having each other to lunch or dinner or meeting at the same shooting parties or other social occasions.

I have grown, over the years, very much to dislike the description 'County Set' which has nowadays all the overtones of self-conscious elitism and exclusivity and which represents something to which it is enviable to belong. A goal for the socially ambitious. I suppose however that it is the nearest I can get to describing the other half of our parents', and increasingly our, lives. It was a world where everyone seemed to live in a castle, or at least a very large house, and owned land in varying quantities which they let off to tenant farmers. They were, in contrast to the evident prosperity of the farming community, all teetering on the verge of bankruptcy as indeed their ancestors had been, if they were to be believed, since time unremembered. Any ostentation or show of wealth was regarded by the *ancien regime* as something to be made mock of.

Unlike Perthshire society which had been touched by the corrosiveness of commercial money, Aberdeenshire still lived in a bygone age. The great families such as the Gordons, the Forbes, the Irvines, the Hays and the Farquharsons were still the great territorial magnates which they had been from the days of clan feudalism.

None of which, in more practical terms, meant anything other than the fact that, in this echelon of society everyone knew everyone else and were most probably connected by old ties of marriage or territorial relationship. This was very far from being part of what is now known as the 'County Set'.

It was more a case of people inheriting a traditional style of living from which they knew no way of escaping nor had they any conscious wish to do so.

Jock Crawford's family house was Rothie Castle – a vast rambling place which could only be reached by a long rutted drive and which had no form of central heating whatever. His father, Colonel Crawford, seemed to us to be really incredibly old and spent most of his days in a high-backed wing chair drawn up close to the fire in the billiards room. His wife, Helena, was very much younger and extraordinarily pretty and vivacious and they fought with each other noisily and constantly. When they went out together in the car, neither was willing to be driven by the other so they had arrived at a compromise. Each journey was mapped out with military precision and a half-way mark agreed between them where the car was stopped and they changed places. There was another thing about Jock's father which intrigued me immensely. It was that he had a pathological fear of dentists. Whenever one of his yellowing fangs became carious, he would pack the cavity with caustic soda and would endure the most dreadful agonies until the caustic soda had cauterized the nerve and the tooth had become dead. Whilst this 'cure' for toothache was in progress Jock told me that his father became totally unbearable. For the rest of the time he was the most kindly and courteous of men. Our visits to Rothie were the greatest fun in the world. They usually lasted all day with the grown-ups playing endless rubbers of bridge. All that was required of us was that we should join them in the big dining room, all gathered closely round the end of a table large enough to seat twenty and then we were free to run wild until, hours later, the blowing of a hunting horn announced that our parents were ready to take their departure.

There could hardly have been a greater contrast between Jock's family and the family of 'Hag' and 'Lag' Gordon. Their father was a retired naval commander and as one might expect a big bluff figure who, even in rare moments of repose, gave the impression that he was striding the quarter deck. He communicated by a series of staccato barks and blew his nose incessantly in a very large red handkerchief. As with Colonel and Mrs Crawford, the contrast between Commander Alastair Gordon and his wife, Gladys, could also hardly have been more extreme. Gladys had the reputation in Aberdeenshire Society of being an extremely fast lady and the reasons were not far to seek. She painted her finger-nails the brightest shade of blue, her face was powdered a mask-like white onto which her mouth and eyes appeared to have been painted by the hand of a surrealist artist. Her dinner parties were the subject of endless, often scandalised, comment although by today's standards they cannot have been much out of the ordinary. I can remember Mum reporting to one of her friends on the telephone that, at one dinner party, there had been *toothpicks* on the table and, what was more, Gladys had used them ostentatiously after every course. More titillating was the rumour that, as a young girl, she had been the mistress of D.H. Lawrence whose book *Lady Chatterley's Lover* was something so scandalous that it could not even be mentioned.

From these two examples it is not difficult to see that the two worlds in which we had our being were so utterly different as to be totally irreconcilable. But from the standpoint of Gordon and myself our friendship with Jock Crawford and Hag and Lag showed marked signs of being only the thin end of the wedge. Everyone in the whole of Aberdeenshire it seemed, who had offspring of around our age, had a compulsion to give parties for them and this *malaise* set in most seriously during the Christmas school holidays.

This did not affect us all that seriously during that first Christmas but it was something which was to gather pace in succeeding years until it reached such proportions as to make the Christmas holidays something to be looked forward to with trepidation.

I have already mentioned that Christmas was not an event which was much celebrated by country folk in those days but I have the most vivid recollections of the New Year celebrations at Tullochford that year.

In contrast to Alton Burn, life on the farm was heaven indeed. Our own stockholding of rabbits and guinea pigs had been reduced almost to extinction because Willie Black the pigman had dug his toes in about undertaking the heavy responsibility of feeding so many mouths which demanded far more attention than even his own demanding animals. There were however many more activities on the farm which required our urgent attention. Not the least of these was the keeping down of the rat population.

I do not know if it was as a result of the decimation of the farm cat population as it had been in Harvey Burr's day but the farm literally swarmed with rats. To go into a hen house to collect the eggs was to find empty eggshells all over the place and, as often as not, disturb a rat or two in the act of making off with eggs out of the nesting boxes. Try as one might to make a store-room rat-proof they would still find a way of frustrating every effort. They gnawed their way through the stoutest timber and even lining the bottoms of the doors with tin had little effect.

Where the rat population was at its thickest and where they bred in the greatest profusion was along the banks of the mill lade. The lade rats were also a distinct species and very much nastier in every way than the ordinary brown rats which had their breeding grounds in the corn stacks in the stack yard and which had, for the most part, only come in from the fields after the harvest. The lade rats were ugly, black and enormous and lived as much in the water as they did in their holes. Then, whenever there was a corn thrashing about to take place in the mill they would crawl in, in what seemed to be their hundreds, from the water wheel and into the engine room. To peer into the semi-darkness was to see them crouched in every corner and even on the machinery itself, patiently waiting.

In those days the destruction of rats was not the comparatively easy matter it is today. There were no selective poisons as we now have so that to scatter rat poison around the place was to risk wiping out most other forms of animal and bird life as well. By and large the corn-stack dwelling rats could be kept under some sort of control but the black water rats were a different kettle of fish. One of our self-appointed tasks those holidays was to be Controllers of Rats.

One of the main products of a corn thrashing was bruised oats. This was corn which had been processed through the bruising machine to make them suitable feed for the horses. For this purpose a separate room was set aside in the mill which housed the bruising machine which was in turn driven by a belt from the engine room. The resulting product formed a small mountain of bruised oats. The smell of freshly bruised oats was a heady smell indeed and totally irresistible to rats.

It was around this scenario that Gordon and I mounted the main thrust of our anti-rat campaign.

There were two doors into the bruiser room; one out of the main body of the mill and the other from the engine room for the driving belt and which was the main access door for the rats. This was our plan, which for devilish cunning took some beating. It was first of all necessary to disconnect the driving belt so that the engine room door could be shut. Then it was necessary to devise a means, by which both doors could be slammed shut simultaneously and operated by remote control. This was achieved by running a long length of binder twine, anchored to the engine room door and thence to the mill-access door and then run the whole length to the main outside door of the mill. By a sharp pull of the binder twine communication cord from the mill door both access doors to the bruiser room could be slammed so that any intruders enjoying a night feast of the bruised oats were irrevocably trapped with no means of escape.

This plan worked a treat. The night following a thrash we would wait, with mounting excitement, until every single rat had the opportunity of getting at the bruised oats. Then we would creep quietly to the barn door, each carrying a blanketed storm lantern and an old tennis racket. Come the sharp tug on the binder twine and the battlefield was set. To reach the bruiser room door, hand by hand along the binder twine and to slip inside was a matter of seconds.

The scene inside by the yellow light cast by the storm

lanterns was like something out of Dante's *Inferno*. There were rats everywhere. Some rushed madly around in panic; others retreated into dark corners from which we could see their eyes gleaming as they crouched ready to spring at the first opportunity.

A tennis racket as an offensive weapon against a rat has it limitations. You can only really take a rat on the move and then it hit it with such force, preferrably against a wall, as to encompass its immediate destruction. A rat cowering in a corner is a difficult, if not an impossible, target. In this matter the rats were generally happy to oblige. Some even took the offensive. They would climb up onto the top of the bruiser and, from this point of vantage, launch themselves to land on the back of our necks whilst we were otherwise engaged in dealing with their companions. A large rat landing on your neck in the dark is not a pleasant experience and we soon learned to keep well clear of the bruiser when our backs were turned.

Although, when first bursting into the small bruiser room, the number of rats always seemed to be legion even a good rat hunt might only produce a bag of a couple of dozen but it still added up to a great number of swipes with a tennis racket. The biggest rat we ever killed measured twenty-six inches from the tip of its nose to the tip of its tail.

That year Dad decided or rather, I suppose, Jimmy Pratt the grieve did, that, as part of the New Year celebrations, a barn dance would be held at the farm. The preparation for this caused the greatest of excitement. Invitations went out by word of mouth to the neighbouring farms that all were welcome and everybody on the farm set to in order to get everything ready for the great night.

The dance was to be held in the loft above the stables and the first priority was get the wooden floor boards into a condition for the tripping of the light fantastic. This entailed repeated applications of a substance called Slipperine which was rubbed into the dance surface-to-be and then polished by a heavy polisher wrapped in sacking. After three or four goings-over, although not perhaps coming up to the standards of a 'Come Dancing' ballroom, the floor took on a pretty good shine. Then all manner of colourful decorations appeared from nowhere. Paper chains and streamers festooned the rafters and covered the stone walls until the long loft began to resemble an embowered grotto.

On the day of the dance the activity rose to fever-pitch. Access to the loft could only be gained by a ladder out of the straw barn and up this mountains of food and drink, not to mention trestle tables and barrels of beer, had to be transported. Goodness knows how, later, the lady guests in all their finery were able to negotiate this final perilous ascent after tripping across the muddy farmyard in their satin slippers I cannot imagine.

The social observances which then obtained at a village dance or even at a barn dance with privately invited guests such as this one were very strict and perhaps worth describing for those unfamiliar with them today, although the customs are still preserved in the more remote parts of Scotland.

The golden rule was that, insofar as it was possible in something so dependent on bodily contact as dancing, the sexes should be kept separated. That is to say that, when not actually gyrating together on the floor they should sit apart for which purpose chairs were provided on opposite sides of the room. Down one side the girls sat demurely with eyes modestly downcast whilst on the other the boys were ranged in their Sunday best, their hair plastered down with brilliantine, and often a flower, embellished with silver paper, carefully arranged in their buttonholes. The moment the music struck up the boys would launch themselves across the floor and, by a backward jerk of the head, indicate to the lady of their choice that it was their wish to favour them with a dance. Then, when the music stopped, each would return to their own side of the room until the next tune was struck up. It was a procedure which could, as the evening wore on, become fraught with drama particularly if two swains were in competition for the same maiden and, conversely, a dreadful agony for any girls not in great demand and whose plight gives rise to the original decription of 'wallflower'.

Even the matrons no longer themselves involved in the battle of the sexes, also sat separate from their menfolk, gossiping together whilst keeping a sharp eye on the goings-on of the young and taking the most careful note of what attentions were paid to who and by whom. No chaperones at a society ball in London could have been more eagle-eyed in their vigilance. For the older men, also in their best turn-out and fingering uncomfortably their unaccustomed collars and ties, it was a rare occasion to discuss such important matters as grain prices and stock yields as well as more domestic matters like who was likely to have hay to spare to carry over to the spring. It was also traditional to arrive each with his own contribution to the festivities in the form of a half bottle or two of whisky, tucked away for convenience in a jacket pocket. As the evening wore on they would slip away into the darkness outside to exchange a dram with their friends, the bottles to be passed to and fro between them and shared in companionable silence before rejoining the fray.

Our barn dance started conventionally with the more decorous exercises of the dance floor such as fox-trots and waltzes, both of the then newly-fashionable cheek-to-cheek variety and the old-fashioned energetic variety of waltz which gave the young men the opportunity of showing off their agility by whirling their partners nearly off their feet. However this was only a preliminary warm-up for the highlights of the evening which were the dancing of reels; Highland Scottiches and other formation dances like the comparatively mild Dashing White Sergeant and that ultimate test of fitness and endurance, Strip the Willow. This was a great treat we had been promised we could stay up for.

At Alton Burn, under the instruction of Lucy Pearson, we had already started to learn the first elements and basic steps of Scottish dancing as an essential part of the social accomplishment of young gentleman but this would have been of no service to us at all that night. There was nothing of the elegantly performed *pas de bas*, the gracious setting to your partner, grand chains or genteel swinging, arms linked, with the left arm held high to shrill cries of 'Teapot! Teapot!' from Lucy.

At the first bow stroke on the fiddle, away everyone went at full gallop, springing and leaping and whirling their partners round with the fanaticism of dancing dervishes whilst giving vent to the wild cries of the clans joining battle in mortal conflict. Surely the sight which greeted Burns' Tam o' Shanter as, on the midnight hour, he peeped through the window of Alloway Kirk could not have been wilder than this.

As the music provided by the two instrumentalists, the fiddler and the accordianist on his 'squeeze box', goaded the dancers on to ever greater efforts and wilder abandon, I saw to my amazement that John Strachan who, with his wife, had been having supper with Mum and Dad, had not only joined in the fray but had taken his turn on the fiddle and was wielding the bow like a man possessed. With the sweat pouring down his face, he set such a pace as to have the bravest dropping from fatigue, as the whole barn rocked from the stamping of feet and the storm lanterns swayed from the rafters.

Long after Gordon and I had been sent protestingly to bed, the skirl of the wild music continued until the clanking of the milk cans announced that another day on the farm had begun.

CHAPTER EIGHT

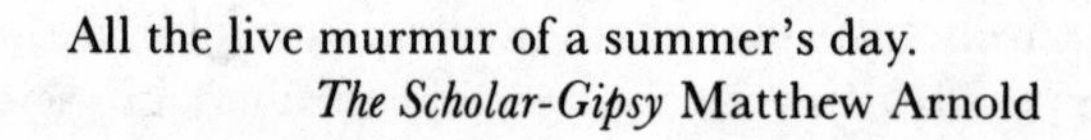

All the live murmur of a summer's day.
The Scholar-Gipsy Matthew Arnold

It is a strange thing that for most of us to look back on summers long gone is to remember them with the sun ever riding high in the sky as the golden days chased one after the other. Certainly that is how I remember them, just as from my childhood I remember all the winters as dark and stormy with snow drifts which blocked us off from the outside world for days at a time and there was skating on the duck pond and chestnuts roasted in a blazing fire for tea.

In summer Alton Burn shed the gaunt image of a penitentiary whose windows gazed out over the grey storm-tossed waters of the Moray Firth, with the surrounding countryside bleak and hostile as far as the eye could see. In spring, the gorse and whin erupted into a sea of yellow blossom, announcing the greening of the landscape to come. The ground across which we had trudged on the wintery days to a distant field, rented from the local farmer to serve as a rugger pitch, started to change by one of Nature's recurring miracles, into a cricket ground, the pitch to be closely mowed and the outfield left lush and verdant. Trees blossomed, birds sang and the roses in N.G.'s rose beds bloomed mightily.

Summer brought with it all manner of special and memorable excitements. Not the least of them was the arrival of the Grand Fleet at Invergordon on the far side of the Cromarty Firth, for summer manoeuvres. The exact date was unpredictable but one morning someone would look out of our dormitory window and shout, 'They're here!' Then we would all crowd to the windows to gaze out at the long grey shapes, lying low and sleek in line ahead, silhouetted against the shoreline of the Black Isle. They were all there: the *Rodney*, the *Hood*, the *Nelson* – all the great men-of-war whose names rang proudly on everyone's lips and whose exploits in the sea battles of the Great War were already legend. There were the cruisers and the destroyers and busy little frigates which had all steamed in from the North Sea during the short hours of darkness to present a thrilling spectacle, riding at anchor with the morning sun glinting on the menacing barrels of their huge guns.

Exciting stuff it was and nobody got more excited by the arrival of the Grand Fleet than Mr MacCarthy. The first lesson would be abandoned whilst we took turns to peer through his private telescope and try to identify, with the help of that great work of reference, Jane's *Fighting Ships*, every vessel down to the very smallest. It was Mr MacCarthy who always took charge of the negotiations which were immediately entered into for the school to be escorted on a visit to the Flagship 'at the invitation of the Admiral' which was the most stupendous of annual summer treats.

Perhaps fortunately, there could hardly have been two people more totally different in outlook and temperament than Mr MacCarthy and Major Pearson. N.G. was a traditionalist of the old school, steeped in the Classics and the Old Testament. His years when he had been through the bloodiest fighting in the trenches and the greatest holocaust in the history of the human race, had left him naively convinced that Right would always triumph over Wrong and Good over Evil.

Mr MacCarthy had been too young for the war but he was looking forward with infectious enthusiasm to life in a land made fit for heroes to live in. It was an enthusiasm which rubbed off on us. I can remember his greeting us at the beginning of one summer term with an account of an amazing adventure in which he had just been closely involved. Mr MacCarthy's parents, with whom he customarily spent his holidays, lived at Ramsgate on the south coast of England. During this Easter vacation he had acquired a spanking new Austin

Seven motor-car and this he had driven, with a companion (later discovered to be the blushing Miss Stewart), all the way back from Ramsgate to Alton Burn, keeping the most precise records of the distances covered each day and the time taken. These statistics were later given to us as an exercise in mathematics to work out his average speed over given distances.

There was one stretch of fifty miles on what was then known as the Great North Road which he and his companion had covered, without even stopping to take on additional petrol, of which he was particularly proud. In those days the Great North Road, now known as the A1, was little better than a country lane but there were some stretches which were reasonably straight and did not run through too many villages.

'Do you know, boys' he told us proudly 'I have worked it out – and you can check this for yourselves – over those fifty miles we averaged just under thirty miles an hour and, I can tell you, there were times when we were driving at speeds of over forty! I believe,' he said, wagging his head solemnly, 'that we may well have set a record which will never be broken.'

Modern technology fascinated him and particularly as it related to speed and speed records. At this time one of the most glamorous events on the calender was the closed-circuit air race for the Schneider Trophy. I am not now sure whether it was Mr MacCarthy's personal enthusiasm for this annual international air race which fired us but I remember looking forward to it and speculating on the chances of the rival nations taking part with far greater attention than was paid to such matters as the outcome of the England versus Australia test series. In the late twenties as I recollect Britain reigned supreme, completing a hat-trick by winning three years in succession and thus gaining ownership of the trophy with the incredible speed of almost 350 mph. 'Man can never fly faster' Mr MacCarthy exulted. 'The human frame would simply disintegrate at any greater speed.'

The 1920s and 30s was also the time of complete domination by Britain in the field of land-speed records. When in 1925 Sir Malcolm Campbell, every schoolboy's hero, established his first world record in his famous Bluebird at 150 mph it was in the eyes of Mr MacCarthy the *ne plus ultra*. I had left Alton Burn by the time, ten years later, when Campbell doubled the record to 301 mph, so I shall never know how Mr MacCarthy came to terms with the impossible happening.

The great thing about Mr MacCarthy was that, so wide-ranging and diverse were his enthusiasms that he could, at the drop of a hat, be diverted from such immensely boring matters as trying to teach us about vulgar fractions or explaining the complexities of long division to dilating at great length on practically anything totally removed from lessons.

There was one splendid occasion when he got off on a tangent which was to occupy us all for the best part of a week. Nairn golf course which is in the class of champion golf courses, ran on the narrow strip of links between the school grounds and the seashore which meant that the outward bound nine holes and the nine holes coming home lay closely alongside each other at many points. Thus it happened that a golfer playing one of the outward bound holes drove his ball off the tee at precisely the same instant as another golfer drove off in the opposite direction from a homeward-bound tee. The first golfer hooked his ball badly and the second pulled his equally badly with the result that the two balls collided in mid-air.

It was of course an astonishing coincidence and the odds against it ever happening again, very long indeed. This was however not nearly good enough for Mr MacCarthy. First of all he had to try and assess exactly how long the odds were. This in turn meant examining all manner of other improbable coincidences in widely differing fields and circumstances. Books of reference were dug out and diligently consulted which led us down fascinating paths of discovery while all pretence of continuing with our arithmetic lessons was abandoned. Then a letter had to be written to the *Scotsman* and we waited daily, with bated breath, to see whether it would appear or not. When it finally did, Mr MacCarthy was so beside himself with excitement that I believe, were it left to him, he would have declared a holiday for the whole school.

Cricket, above all school games, was a passion with N.G.

Most summer evenings he would have us all out for fielding practice or batting in the nets. One of the troubles was that there were not many school sides for us to play against. The nearest school which could field a side of our own age was Fort Augustus, a distinguished Roman Catholic school which was over on the West Coast right at the far end of the Caledonian Canal, at Fort William. This meant a bus journey to Inverness and then the long drive down Loch Ness which must be one of the most beautiful and dramatic drives in all Scotland. As the world now knows, Loch Ness is famous as the abode of the Loch Ness Monster who single-handed has done more for Scotland's tourist trade than all the spectacular scenery, castles and ancient legends put together. In fact 'Nessie' was only 'discovered' during my third summer term at Alton Burn. The effect this had on Mr MacCarthy cannot be hard to imagine. It also made our coach drives to play cricket or rugger against Fort Augustus even more charged with drama than they already were.

Quite apart from its famous monster, Loch Ness is one of the most sinister and enigmatic lochs in Scotland or probably anywhere else in Europe. It is enormously deep – over a thousand feet – and part of the geological fault known as the Great Rift where, before the Ice Age, there was a sideways slip of the land mass, the crack nearly severing the country into two. The mountains rising sharply on either side of the dark waters which culminate with Ben Nevis, Scotland's highest peak, on the south side, plunge so steeply below water level as to make the sides almost vertical. In the depths there are shelves of rock running back far under the hillsides and, so it is said, connected with a subterranean fault which re-appears as far south as the Iberian Peninsular. As proof of this, and we had this on the authority of Mr MacCarthy himself, whenever there is an earth tremor in Spain or Portugal, it affects the level of the waters of Loch Ness. It is said that at the time of the great earthquake of 1755 which destroyed most of Lisbon in Portugal the level rose by over ten feet.

Much more gripping to the imagination however is that these

shelves are the lairs of gigantic eels which gives rise to the theory that the monster, or monsters, may be just eels grown to mammoth size over the centuries or prehistoric survivors from the time of the land slip. The existence of these eels is vouched for by an event which occurred just before the Great War. A certain titled lady was being rowed on the loch when by some mischance an extremely valuable pearl necklace which she was wearing slipped from her neck and fell into the water quite near to the shore – near enough for an attempt to be made to recover the necklace by the use of divers. A deep-sea diver went down but, before many minutes, he was signalling violently to be brought up again. In a state of gibbering terror he reported that he had come upon these enormous eels in such quantity and of such ferocious appearance that nothing would induce him to go down again. All very good stuff for the schoolboy imagination. How much of it is strictly true is something that I would not dream of enquiring into. Many years later, passing by Fort Augustus, I paid a call on the Abbot, a man of high theological reputation as well as comfortable worldliness. Sitting in his splendid study which commanded a view up Loch Ness, I thought to ask him whether he had ever seen the famous monster. 'Almost every day of my life' he replied solemnly.

The great cricketing event of the summer was the Fathers' Match which took place at half term. The Fathers' team, captained by N.G. himself, were handicapped by having to bat with 'broomsticks' – a cricket bat cut down to the size of a baseball bat which usually resulted in their ignominious rout at the hands of the boys. The greatest fun was to be had from our point of view, however, in seeing what other boys' parents looked like for, of course, all the mothers were there too, dressed in their very finest. Looking back now, I remember with some surprise just how critical we were. For the rest of the year parents were – well, just parents whom we took for granted. There was nothing much one could do about them anyway. They had to be written to every Sunday in term time and who, one hoped, during the holidays did not interfere too much with one's own pursuits.

For some reason when they came on visits to take us out, which they were allowed to do twice a term, we all became desperately keen that they should show up well in front of the other boys as well as refraining from doing anything embarrassing like hugging or kissing – at least in public. At the Fathers' Match this was all doubly important. It was not simply just how they looked and how they behaved; it was what cars they arrived in and that they should not bring hangers-on with them such as younger brothers or, much worse, sisters.

During the whole time I was at Alton Burn there were only two families who were town dwellers and, in each case, they were two brothers. One of their fathers was a prominent estate agent in Edinburgh and the other a Glasgow stockbroker. Both of them came in for quite a bit of ragging after being visited by their respective parents on the grounds that they were, not to put too fine a point on it, flashy. The cars they arrived in were, if not in the Rolls-Royce class which would have been unforgiveable, large and shiny and the stockbroker in particular was given to expansive gestures like presenting cups for things. One of the cups he gave to be presented which really took the biscuit was for The Most Popular Boy in the School. Every boy was required to write an essay in support of his candidate with the proviso only that you could not vote for yourself. When on the first year in which it was presented I won the wretched thing, with myself as the only dissenter, my embarrassment was total and lasting.

One of the troubles, amongst many obvious advantages of being such a small school was when it came to team games played amongst ourselves. With cricket, if the school was at full strength, it was possible to raise two elevens with every boy on parade but with rugger which required teams of fifteen-a-side this was not a possibility. There was also the consideration that the boys varied in age from seven years old to twelve and the difference in size and physique at that age is formidable indeed. For a seven-year-old to attempt to tackle a twelve-year-old thundering down the wing in possession of the ball is not a very practical proposition. Nonetheless N.G., with his obsession with encouraging the competitive spirit in everything and everybody, insisted on teams being made up to vie with each other daily on the playing fields. This led to a form of team selection which, from very early on in my time at Alton Burn, I found obnoxious. At the very beginning of each term N.G. appointed captains and vice-captains of everything. At the beginning of each game all the school was assembled in their playing kit when the captain and vice-captain picked opposing sides by calling out the name of a boy alternately for his team. This meant that the smaller or the generally more useless boy was always left to last, looking more and more abject and unwanted as every boy in the school was selected ahead of him. When, in my due turn, I became captain of everything, I introduced a system whereby names for opposing teams were drawn out of a hat. That this, on occasions, resulted in one team consisting entirely of boys with pretensions as bowlers and the others as batsmen still made it in my opinion a more humane, if perhaps a less efficient, system.

The other great summer event was the school sports which were held in the last week of term. There can be nothing more competitive than athletics; nor any sporting activity where the prize goes to the most highly trained and to the one with the finest physical equipment. That some of us had longer legs than others or more developed muscles was in part overcome by the school dividing into two classes: the seven to tens and the tens to twelves. This had the satisfactory result that with approximately ten boys in each section, competing with each other in six or seven different events, it was extraordinarily difficult for any boy, however physically disadvataged, not to gain some sort of distinction even if it was only to come third in the long jump in his age group. Every term N.G. produced a very smart looking school magazine which reported every happening in the greatest detail and the school sports results always took up two or three closely written pages in which any boy would be unlucky if he did not feature somewhere.

I can remember after one summer term when Gordon and I were as was usual spending part of the holidays with Granny at Wester Kinloch, showing Lizzie the school magazine. She read this with the closest attention, her spectacles perched on the end of her nose as she followed each report line by line, her lips moving soundlessly. It so happened that that term Gordon, being the most athletic if not the biggest amongst the seniors, and I, enjoying a similar advantage in the juniors, had each won every single event in our respective sections except for one odd event amongst the seniors in which Gordon for some reason had only come second. When Lizzie had finished her perusal, she removed her glasses and looking Gordon straight in the eye, demanded sternly, 'Hoo did ye nae win throwin' the cricket ba'?'

Another activity reserved for the summer term and by which N.G. set the greatest store, was rifle shooting. Convinced as he was that the next war was only round the corner, he felt it as his patriotic duty to see that we were as fully prepared as we could be to defend our country when the call came. For this purpose the school was affiliated to an organisation called the Junior Empire League and one of the requirements of membership was that all of us should, at as early an age as possible, learn to handle firearms. N.G. had in the grounds of his cottage adjoining the school grounds, created a small rifle range where we took turns to learn the skills of target shooting with a ·22 air-rifle. Once we had reached the required standard of proficiency each boy was awarded a medal with a splendid ribbon in red, white and blue. One of N.G.'s wilder ideas was that each boy who had won a medal should wear it on his kilt jacket in which we went to church on Sundays but that was eventually quashed, I think at the request of the minister, and a compromise reached by which we could only wear the medal on Empire Day.

Church attendance on Sunday – Church Parade as it was called – was another field in which N.G.'s love of regimentation could be given full rein. Sunday was the only day on which we wore kilts. Each boy was required to bring a kilt to school in whatever family tartan he might be entitled to. It was also required that he bring a rug for his bed, also in the family tartan. As there were no boys at the school who were not Scottish this did not present any problem until one term when we had a Russian amongst the intake but that is something I will come to later. All the boys belonged either to the Church of Scotland or to the Scottish Episcopal Church. My mother was an Episcopalian and I honestly do not think my father either knew or cared which he belonged to. In fact there should have been no doubt at all in his mind as the Reverend Thomas Chalmers (my second name is Chalmers), whose statue stands proudly in George Street in Edinburgh and to which the City's pigeons pay daily tribute, is an ancestor and he is the founder of the Scottish Free Church. Thus N.G., himself a stauch Presbyterian, had no difficulty in deciding where my and Gordon's affiliations lay.

On Sunday morning we all paraded in our Sunday best and formed into two squads. Then each boy was issued with one penny to put in his sporran to be kept safe until the collection plate came round. The Episcopalians formed ranks and were marched off first under the command of Mr MacCarthy, they having to go further, followed by our lot with N.G. marching in front of his men and looking back over his shoulder from time to time as if to make sure that none of us had broken ranks. The distance was rather over two miles with the last bit of it through the streets of Nairn. We must have made a brave show as we swung along, lacking only a pipe band.

N.G. took every opportunity to make much of the differences in our religious denominations, quite often organising games and competitions of various sorts between the 'Piskys' and the 'Presbys' which we all took in good part:

'Pisky-Pisky-Palians! Down on your knees and up again!' we would all chant from the school windows as they arrived back after us, mocking them for their practice of kneeling for prayers which was not done in the Presbyterian Church. In fact the Presbyterian services were excruciatingly dull, with the intoning of seemingly endless Paraphrases and Psalms and seldom enlivened by the hell-fire sermons of the old ministers. When I eventually went on to my next school, Trinity College,

Glenalmond, which was the highest of high church, I found the services in the school chapel which we were required to attend every morning and evening and for twice as long on Sundays to be much more to my taste.

To mention the penny given to us each Sunday to put on the church collecting plate (always a plate, never a bag, in Presbyterian churches so that tight-wads could be easily spotted! N.G. always put in a shining-new half crown which impressed us enormously) is to remind me that in our childhood we never handled money. That is to say there was no such thing as pocket money. When we did have the occasional windfall, we would completely lose our heads.

I can remember well one such occasion during the holidays. We had all been invited as a family for lunch by a charming, rather reclusive old couple called Duff at Meldrum House* which was just outside the village of Old Meldrum. After lunch our host slipped us *each* half-a-crown in, I suppose, the vague hope that we would clear off somewhere and leave the grown-ups to an hour or so of peace.

No sooner were we outside the front door than we were down the long drive and off to the village a further mile away where we burst, hot and excited, into Mr Guillanotti's ice-cream parlour. At that time there could hardly have been a village in all Scotland which did not boast an Italian ice-cream parlour which sold every conceivable kind of confection and served as the social centre for the village youth.

My first investment was in six Mars Bars, then very much larger than they are today, which at two pence each represented a whole shilling of my working capital. Then there followed a shopping spree as reckless as that of any latter-day housewife at the January sales, with Gordon equally carried away in a fever of spending. Prudently, before presenting ourselves all wide-eyed and innocent in the drawing room at Meldrum House, we concealed our loot in the boot of Dad's motor-car, later to be smuggled up to our bedroom to provide the makings of much

* Now the Meldrum House Hotel.

midnight feasting for nights afterwards. Whether, when I read of the vast weekly amounts of money which parents nowadays apparently dish out to their children, it teaches them financial prudence, I do not know. All I do know is that I have remained totally irresponsible about money all my life.

There was another aspect of my childhood which may now seem strange to modern eyes. It was that, until I was into my teens, I never really knew anyone of my age of the opposite sex. All the females in my life had been grown-ups and, although I may have been vaguely aware that they were constructed differently from males, it was not really something of which I took very much notice. Sex with a capital 'S' was, of course, something which had not yet impinged on my consciousness nor had it, so far as I know, on the consciousness of any of my companions. I do, however, remember the amazement, not to say amusement, of us all whenever we played the boys at Fort Augustus and shared a changing room with them afterwards, at observing that they all covered their private parts with a little pouch – a *cache-sex* I think it is called. It was part of their Catholicism and worn presumably lest the sight of another boy's genitals might, even at that early age, drive them wild with desire.

Certainly too we were, in a sort of light-hearted way, conscious of our own bodies. In the dorm we used to indulge in a practice called 'showing sights'. A boy, coming back from his bath clad only in his dressing gown, would open it to give us all a quick flash and this was considered to be greatly daring. There was also, after lights-out, sometimes a little bed-hopping and perhaps a furtive fumble or two but the purpose was mostly to exchange whispered confidences.

We also used to examine each others bottoms after a caning but this was purely so that an opinion could be passed as to whether N.G.'s technique was improving or otherwise. There was, however, another aspect of corporal punishment which, at the time, raised in us an unusual indignation.

'Bratter' Gordon who was one of my exact contemporaries and close ally, was a compulsive bed-wetter. I think quite a few new boys suffered from this inconvenience initially, probably as a result of sheer nerves. Bratter, however, the most intrepid and happy-go-lucky of boys, simply could not break the habit. As the term progressed and his bed each morning resembled nothing more than the Yellow Sea, the problem became one for the distaff side and as such the responsibility of N.G.'s wife, Lucy. Her philosophy, it was to appear, was identical with N.G's. Where N.G. took the view that if, any boy was backward in his lessons it was entirely due to lack of application and general idleness and nothing that could not be cured by a good beating, so Lucy took the view that Bratter's malfunction was simply evidence of a perversity over which he had perfect control should he wish to exercise it.

The result of this was that Lucy took to creeping into our dorm at some late hour in the night and ripping the clothes off Bratter's bed. Should she find that he had wet himself she would then haul him out of bed and take him down to her sitting room where she would remove his soaking pyjama trousers and, bending him over the piano stool, beat him furiously with her slipper. Bratter, whose bum had become hardened as a result of many disagreements with N.G., felt little pain but was totally enraged by the indignity of it all and we all agreed with him. It was no part of the role of women to take little boys' trousers off and beat their bottoms with a slipper. (It occurs to me in the present climate that this might be held to be a classic case of child abuse.)

Nor did our schoolboy humour show any evidence of sex-orientated sniggering. It relied heavily on the 'what's-the-difference-between' type of joke. Example:

'What is the difference between a dead bee and a sick elephant?'

'I don't know.'

'A dead bee is a bee deceased and a sick elephant is a seedy beast.'

Another example:

'What is the difference between an elephant and a postage stamp?'

'I don't know.'

'Remind me never to ask you to go and buy a postage stamp.'

Stories like these set us rocking in the aisles but it was as nothing when compared with the very rare sit-com. type of story which boys sometimes came back with after the holidays. This one has stuck in my mind:

There were two maiden ladies sitting together having tea in the garden when – a rare event indeed – an aeroplane passed high over their heads.

'I think' said one lady to the other, 'That that must be a mail plane.'

'Don't be so silly' retorted the other 'Those are only the wheels.'

Whilst this story demonstrates a certain awareness of anatomical detail, it can hardly come into the category of sexual smut! Nor could it have any relevance in these jet-propelled days!

There was, however, one incident which I would like to record which happened during the last summer term I spent at Alton Burn and which might be properly regarded as the beginning of my sexual emancipation.

Between the school grounds and the golf course there was a wide swathe of whin bushes through which paths ran, which gave access to small natural glades. It was a favourite diversion for the townsfolk of Nairn to stroll there of a summer's evening and a great favourite with the young intent on romantic dalliance. One evening two or three of us were lounging by an open upper window as dusk started to fall, enjoying the cool air after another blazingly hot day, when we noticed a young couple in close embrace in one of the small clearings in the bushes right in front of us. Then, even as we watched, the young man proceeded to remove his jacket and, arranging it carefully on the ground, indicated to his paramour that they should recline upon it – a suggestion with which she complied with the greatest alacrity.

'Good heavens!' exclaimed Charlie Scott-Moncrieff suddenly,

peering into the gathering dusk, 'I do believe he is taking off her knickers!'

And so it certainly appeared. When, shortly afterwards they started rolling together on the grass with the lady's silk-clad legs performing all manner of gymnastics in the air, somebody said: 'What on earth are they up to now?'

'I think,' said Felix de Hamel, one of the more sophisticated amongst us and who sometimes spent his holidays in France, 'that perhaps he is trying to give her a baby.'

I must say that I was absolutely thunderstruck. All manner of pictures flashed through my mind. I do not think that life back at the farm was ever quite the same again after that.

Yes, certainly the summer was the best part of the scholastic year. And so, increasingly were the summer holidays to come.

CHAPTER NINE

> . . . fishing I can only compare to a stick and a string, with a worm at one end and a fool at the other.
>
> Remark attributed to
> Doctor Samuel Johnson.

Our devotion to fishing was not something, oddly enough, which Gordon and I shared with any boys we knew of our age. Neither of Jimmy Pratt's boys, nor their contemporaries from the farms round about, were in the least bit interested in the art of tempting the wily little brown trout into giving themselves up although Jocky did go through a phase of trying to catch eels. This he did by setting night lines for them, borrowing I may say for the purpose not only our hooks but helping himself to our valuable and carefully nurtured worms.

I have already remarked on the important part played by the worm in the capture of the fish and the attention which should be paid to getting the right worm for the job. It did not, however, as we soon found out, stop there. Our advisor on these matters was Willie Black, a bachelor who lived on his own and worked one of the crofts behind Tullochford. At the same time he was also available for any seasonal jobs around the farm and was a man who could turn his hand to anything. The proper care of worms was one of his specialities.

It was Willie who first pointed out the folly of digging a prime brandling out of the midden, sticking it on a hook and dropping it under a trout's nose and trusting it not to help itself to a free meal without getting itself hooked. To put an unmatured worm on the hook was simply to ask for this to happen. Worms, declared Willie, have to be matured like good wine and this is done by storing them in a tin packed with slightly damp moss until they get rid of all the waste matter in their bodies and become tough. During this process they must also be able to breathe and for this purpose holes should be hammered, by use of a nail, into the lid of the tin. The first time we obeyed these instructions and put the tins for safety under our beds, all the worms squeezed out during the night so that when Nurse Webster (who still put herself in charge of us during the holidays), came into our room in the morning there were worms everywhere, all over the carpets, climbing up the walls and leaving trails of slime on the furniture. After that, although we modified the size of the holes, we were banned from bringing worms into the house and had to leave them in the stables where Jocky had access to them for his eel catching exploits.

Amongst other pieces of folklore propounded by Jocky Pratt was one about eels. It was said that if you plucked a white hair from the tail of a horse and secured it with a stone on the bed of a stream, left overnight it would be found in the morning to have turned into a silver eel. Naturally we tried out this theory many times but we were never successful. I am convinced however that there is in every superstition (or call it what you will) a basis of fact. The life cycle of the eel is a fascinating one. All eels which pour in their millions as elvers up every freshwater river and tiny stream all over Europe, have floated across the Atlantic on the Gulf Stream from their common place of birth deep down in the mysterious waters below the floating mass of seaweed which forms the Sargasso Sea in the Gulf of Mexico. They remain in their chosen waters, gorging themselves on whatever they can find for up to seven years. Then, one night when the moon is full, they are seized with the instinct to return to their birthplace, there to recreate and die. From that moment they cease to eat, all the vents in their bodies close up and their bellies turn from yellow to bright silver.

How easy to believe, before the days of scientific explanation, that a migrating eel, turned suddenly silver, had indeed started out its life as a white hair from a horse's tail.

There is a certain feyness about the Scottish nature which is not exactly superstition but more a willingness to believe things which cannot be described as having the authority of hard scientific fact. A good example of this is the acceptance, particularly amongst farming communities of those days, of the power of the 'horseman's word'.

The horseman's word is something which is known only to a very few. It is passed on from one horseman to another and is a secret more closely guarded than any in even the most arcane practices of freemasonry.

Those who know the secret word are the possessors of great power for, whispered to a horse, it has the power of rendering the wildest and most intractable animal as quiet and docile as a lamb. Tommy Rendall, our head cattleman who had followed Dad down from Stronsay claimed that, although he did not know the word himself, his father had known it and his father before him and there was no doubt that everyone to do with the horses at Tullochford, including Jimmy Pratt himself, believed implicitly in the existence of the word. Or, at least, so they assured Gordon and me.

Not many years ago I read of a lady in England who claimed and in fact could demonstrate a remarkable power over horses. This she could exercise by simply breathing into the horse's nostrils. I wonder if she was whispering the horseman's word or, to be more practical, did breathing soothingly up a horse's nostrils have a calming effect on the animal? I prefer to believe the former.

But I have wandered rather from our passion for fishing. As I have said it was something none of our friends shared and not even my greatest friend at the time, Jock Crawford, despite the fact that the Rothie Burn, which ran through the grounds of Rothie Castle on its way to join the River Ythan, was positively teeming with trout and much larger ones than we could boast on our own home waters.

When we got back from school for the summer holidays

the first thing we did, pausing only to divest ourselves of our school uniforms which were consigned to the back of the deepest cupboard we could find, was to get out our rods and tackle and start planning our campaign against old and wily adversaries and to discover new and hitherto untried pastures. This latter was something over which both our parents, in their individual ways, were to give us rather unexpected support.

It became traditional over the years that we should spend the first part of the summer holidays in Perthshire at Wester Kinloch and this suited us really very well. There was only one snag so far as I was concerned and that was the car journey which it entailed. The distance was over a hundred miles and I knew that we would scarcely have gone twenty before I started to get car sick. Maddeningly Gordon was not afflicted in the same way and this gave me a serious inferiority complex which was not helped by Dad's attitude which was a mixture of impatience and disbelief that there was anything the matter at all. To have to drive such an enormous distance was bad enough in itself without unnecessary complications of my making. Nothing short of my throwing up all over the back seat would cause him to stop and by then it was anyhow too late.

Once we had got to Aberdeen there were two routes we could take to reach Blairgowrie. One route was down the coast road and through the rich but dull agricultural countryside of the Mearns, immortalised in the writings of Lewis Grassic Gibbon*. The other, and much more exciting road, followed the course of the River Dee past the Royal estate of Balmoral and then, once over the foothills of the Grampians, dropped steeply down again to below the snow line by way of the notorious Devil's Elbow which was then little more than a roughly-metalled hill track twisting and turning round hair-raising bends. The excitement of taking this road had the effect of completely banishing my car sickness. The sight of broken-down or blown-up motor cars every few miles was

* Author of *A Scots Quair: Sunset Song* 1932, *Cloud Howe* 1933, *Grey Granite* 1934. He was born in 1901 and died in 1935.

infinitely preferable to the monotonous progress past the regular white milestones which marked every step of the way through the flat lands. Either way I have never had much time for the dictum that it is better to travel hopefully than to arrive.

Although in years ahead Kinloch was to assume the role of my family home, during all the years of my childhood it retained a certain quality of unreality. Tullochford was always in my mind the real life and the safe place to escape back to from the perils of schooldays. I looked forward to visits to Kinloch as a sort of holiday within the holidays where one lived out of a suitcase and never really got unpacked.

Granny, despite being very conscious of social position, was not herself a very social person although, when we came to stay, she would make an effort and take us out to tea at some of the large houses round about with whom she remained on visiting terms. This, of course, was almost total agony for us although we did rather enjoy visits to Glamis Castle with its legends of ghosts and a monster who was kept in a hidden room with the heir only told the secret on his coming of age. That it was the scene of the murder of Macbeth was much more exciting than the fact that it was the birthplace of the future Queen Mother, despite our tenuous relationship with the family of which Granny was so proud.

That is not to say that our visits to Kinloch were not the greatest fun, what with going out after pike on the loch and a multitude of other fascinating ploys, as well as, of course, having Lizzie fussing over us like a mother hen and all the attention paid to our every whim.

I have already remarked that our parents led a very social life in which we by and large had taken little part but, as we grew older, that started to change. From our point of view this was something to be deplored were it not for one aspect of this new development of which we approved mightily. Because visiting what were classed as neighbours often entailed quite considerable journeys of thirty miles or more, it was usual to go for the day or even, if a dinner party was involved, to stay overnight. As everyone lived in very large houses this did not present any domestic difficulties but, more importantly from the point of view of Gordon and myself, it meant that we would usually be invited to enjoy whatever sporting facilities their estates had to offer.

Of all the houses where we went the one top of the popularity list was Drum Castle*, the ancient family seat of the Irvine family who had lived there in unbroken line since the lands had orginally been granted to them by King Robert the Bruce in the fourteenth century. It was one of the oldest inhabited castles in Scotland as well as one of the friendliest and most cosy of houses. In spite of its antiquity it was one of the very few castles which did not boast a ghost of any kind until my mother claimed to have seen one – but then my mother always saw a ghost whatever house she stayed in. She claimed to have what is known as the 'second sight'.

More important to us than all this was that Drum had some of the finest fishing on that most majestic of rivers, the Aberdeenshire Dee. It extended to almost two miles and was divided into three beats of which the Upper and Lower were let and Sandy Irvine kept the middle water where he entertained his friends most royally during the fishing season. The Dee is of course famous as one of the finest of all salmon rivers but that was something to which Gordon and I had yet to graduate. On the other hand to worm for trout on such grand water was hardly the done thing and it was here that we first learnt the higher skills of fly fishing. Our mentor was Robb who had been the ghillie at Drum ever since Sandy Irvine's father's day. To us he soon became the most tried and trusted of friends. I make no excuse for digressing here briefly to describe this most remarkable of men.

Robb – nobody knew him as anything but Robb – was cut in the true Scottish mould, stockily built and rugged, with the kindly, weathered face of a man equally at home in the great outdoors or round the hospitable hearth with a convivial glass

* Now the property of the National Trust for Scotland.

in his hand. He also had a cork leg which was something which intrigued us greatly and which had replaced his own which had been shot off during the Battle of Mons. Nobody could tie a fly, cast a line or gaff a fish with greater dexterity than Robb. His kingdom was the river bank and the fishing hut his castle and he ruled his domain with all the authority of a feudal lord, knuckling the forehead to none. Should he feel that the guests were lingering overlong over the splendid lunchtime hospitality provided in the fishing hut, he never minced words sending them about their business:

'Awa' oot o' here an' doon the watter, the lot o' ye! Ye'll niver catch a fush in a glais o'whusky' was his war-cry and out everyone would obediently troop. 'Not you, your ladyship' he is once supposed to have said to the Marchioness of Huntly, 'I'm needin' you to bide here tae do the washing-up.'

Robb's weakness was his love of the bottle and there were occasions when he got 'overtaken wi' the drink'. Once when called down the river bank to help land a fish, instead of doing so with his usual efficiency, he himself fell into the river. 'Thank goodness for his cork leg' Sandy said cheerfully, 'otherwise he would have sunk like a stone.'

Robb had his favourites and others of the fishing guests whom he did not like with quite the same warmth. In the latter category was the Colonel who was at that time commanding the depot of the Gordon Highlanders at Brig o' Don. He was an extrordinarily bad-tempered man whose bite, according to other officers under his command, was even worse than his bark. He barked at Robb once too often. It happened one freezing February morning that the Colonel was fishing the top stretch which required, when the water was high, the negotiation of a plank which served as a bridge across to what became an island. Robb, who was ghillieing for the Colonel, saw to it that the plank was firmly in place before the Colonel ventured to cross over but it somehow tipped up when he was on it and he finished up in six feet of icy water. 'There maun hae been some ice on the plank' Robb explained complacently.

It was up by the island that I had one of my earliest fishing triumphs. It was a very hot summer's day and the water was so low you could nearly wade across the river. Sandy had a full complement of guests, flogging away in a rather half-hearted manner. With my trout rod I wandered up to the island, now not an island at all in the low water but where there was some nice rushy water, and just the place to try a wet fly for a trout or two. I was casting away happily with not much doing when there was a considerable splash and I was into a salmon! It was quite a moment in a boy's life.

It is a tricky business landing a heavy fish on light tackle and my life was made no more easy by the fact that I had, unaccountably, a knot in my line which, every time I managed to get the fish reeled in, threatened to get stuck in the top ring of the rod so that a sudden rush would inevitably result in a break. To add to my troubles I had no landing net capable of coping with an emergency such as this. Anyway as it happened success attended upon my efforts. When finally I had the exhausted fish flapping on in the shallows, I cast my rod aside and threw myself upon it, getting thoroughly soaked in the process. Seconds later I had my first salmon safely on dry land. It was a splendid clean-run fish of just seven and a half pounds. Not by any means a big fish, certainly by Dee standards, but to me who had never hitherto caught a trout above a pound in weight, a veritable monster.

I floated the half mile back to the fishing hut on a pink cloud of delight to be greeted with a mixture of astonishment and congratulation – it was the only salmon to have been caught that week – save only by the irascible colonel who could hardly conceal his chagrin and envy, even to the length of suggesting that the salmon could not have been taken by fair means where upon Robb sharply advised him to 'haud his blether' or, to put it more politely, shut his face.

Sandy was totally delighted and duly blooded me on the forehead and both cheeks. Needless to say I did not wash for a week.

Dad very seldom came to the Drum fishing parties. They were much more Mum's scene. She was an expert salmon fisher and had the distinction of once landing a fish of over forty pounds – a 'portmanteau' fish, as salmon of that size were known and rather less rare on rivers like the Dee, the Tay and the Tweed than they are today. It was still a remarkable feat for a woman and raises the question which is still debated today as to whether women are lucky or simply better anglers.

In this connection it might be interesting to mention another house where we used to go to fish. This was Mountblairy, a wonderful sporting estate near Huntly owned by a great friend of Dad's, Captain Alec Morison and where Dad used to go and stay mainly for the shooting. The Mountblairy fishing was on the Deveron, then a prime salmon and trout river which, alas, like so many others has suffered a sharp decline since the last war because of all the ills to which wildlife has become the heir due, in large part, to 'improved' farming methods.

Alec Morison was another man in my armoury of childhood heroes. I cannot ever remember him dressed other than in ancient, almost ragged tweeds with his drooping moustaches yellowed with the nicotine of innumerable cigarettes. He and his wife, Tiny, had no children and they lived in their vast mausoleum of a house with only a scattering of servants to look after them. Alec was a rather reclusive man and I think never happier than when on the river bank with a rod in his hand or wandering round his large estates with a gun under his arm. He was, above all things, a trout fisherman and would spend hours with Gordon and me on the banks of the Deveron pointing out likely lies for a fish and watching us with a critical eye as we cast a fly over them.

It is to his wife, Tiny, that goes the distinction of catching the largest salmon ever caught in British waters on a fly. Very shortly after this record had been established, Miss Valentine, the daughter of the head ghillie on the Glendelvine water of the Tay, caught a still larger salmon but this was caught on a bait. The story of Jessie Valentine's monster fish and of the fight it put up (lasting some three and a half hours) is well recorded. I knew her well. Glendelvine is a neighbouring estate to Kinloch and I have heard the details of the epic battle many times from her own mouth.

Alec Morison died when we were still at Alton Burn and left Gordon and me all his guns and fishing tackle. He also left it in his will that he was to be cremated and his ashes scattered in his favourite fishing pool. Tiny however decided that this would perpetuate too many sentimental memories and followed instead his alternative request that his ashes be put down a rabbit hole.

After Alec's death Gordon and I frequently went to stay with Tiny on our own in the cottage on the estate into which she moved, looked after only by Watson, the gamekeeper, and his wife. It was then that she told us the story of her own great salmon.

She had been fishing all morning with their old ghillie and Tiny already had two salmon on the bank and the ghillie, who was fishing alongside her, one. There is a long slack stretch of water in the middle of the Mountblairy beat and she was idly casting at the top of it. She had just remarked how seldom this water produced a fish when there was a sharp tug on her line. She struck and what was obviously a large fish headed off ponderously, underwater for the main stream. It was a fairly half-hearted attempt and less than ten minutes later a great black brute of a fish with an ugly hooked jaw tamely gave itself up. Unlike Miss Valentine's splendid fresh-run fish, Tiny's must have been in fresh water for a very long time and obviously lost all its *joie de vivre*!

Tiny, herself a very shy and retiring person, was totally embarrassed by all the publicity her 'feat' evoked, at the time even to the extent of being reluctant to have a cast made of the fish.*

There was one other invitation to fish to which we looked forward with great eagerness during the holidays. Although

* The cast is now in the possession of my brother, Gordon, to whom she bequeathed it.

the circumstances under which we were invited were rather different, they did not in any way mitigate our enjoyment.

Dad was a man of many parts. He was fully ten years older than my mother yet, under the rather austere face which he presented to the world, there beat the young heart of the true romantic. I think it must have been my mother who, in their courting days, gave him the nickname of 'Cupid'. Anyone less like the accepted conception of Cupid it would be hard to imagine; nonetheless the name stuck and he continued to be known by the abbreviated form of 'Cup' (pronounced 'Quep') all his life. Handsome he undoubtedly was, despite his pre-occupation with his thinning hairlne and the trim of his military moustache and there was no doubt that the ladies went for him in a big way.

One of his most ardent admirers was a lady called Ivy Patterson who was the wife of Walter Patterson, a retired businessman who had acquired a great fortune in Celyon during the 1914–18 War and who had bought a splendid house called Place of Tillifourie on the banks of another of Aberdeenshire's great rivers, the Don, with a lot of land, including a very good grouse moor.

It may be pertinent to remark here that anybody who had made a great deal of money during the war was generally held to be *persona non grata.* Walter Patterson's background was impeccable, he had played rugger for Scotland and cricket for Ceylon where he had made his considerable fortune in, I think, tea. But he had not 'done his stuff' like everyone else in the war and was firmly stuck with the label of being a War Profiteer. Aberdeenshire with its hierarchy of large traditional landowners was reactionary over matters like this and I believe he was actually blackballed for membership of the Northern Club in Aberdeen – the ultimate snub.

Ivy Patterson was an Australian whom he had met in Ceylon and who had an international reputation as a violinist and was an extraordinarily beautiful woman to boot. As I have hinted she was rather more than a close friend of Dad's. The Pattersons had a very beautiful daughter, Lorna, who became one of the first girlfriends if it merits such a description, of my boyhood. Any aspirations I may have had in this respect when I was in my late teens came to an end when she got herself abruptly married, at a very tender age, to a soldier called Orde Wingate who was to become Major General Orde Wingate, Commander of the Chindits in the Battle for Burma and a dedicated supporter of the aspirations of the Jews in Palestine before his tragic death in an air crash.

It was perhaps not entirely for unselfish reasons that Dad went to great trouble to arrange frequent days fishing at Tilliefourie and which entailed him giving up so much of his own time to take us over there. This did not matter, nor indeed occur, to us. The trout fishing in those days on the Don was in the very top class.

CHAPTER TEN

Come hither, come hither, come hither:
Here shall he see
No enemy
But winter and rough weather.
As You Like It William Shakespeare

There could be no greater contrast for Gordon and me than the delights of our summer holidays and those of the winter and, as time went on, these differences became more and more marked.

For those brought up in the towns, the changing seasons cannot have the same impact as they do on the country-bred. It is not just a matter of the exciting glitter of Christmas shopping with, hopefully, lots of jolly parties to be set against the equally exciting prospect of expeditions to the seaside with bucket and spade. In the country the whole tempo is different but this was certainly more true of the comparatively remote country districts as they were sixty years ago. Nor I am sure is it only in my imagination that the changing seasons were more clearly defined than they are today. Certainly the summers may not have been bathed in constant sunshine as I remember them but that the winters were more wintery does not seem to me to be open to doubt.

The Christmas holidays saw days on end when we were snowed in. This could happen with extraordinary suddenness. To go to bed one night with the roads clear and only a few powdery snowflakes falling was not to say that one would not wake up the following morning to a countryside inches deep in snow and, if the slightest wind had got up, the drifts of snow against the hedges at the sides of the road could be ten feet deep and more.

I can remember one incident which illustrates this and which caused all concerned some amusement at the time. Well, perhaps not at the exact time it happened but when those most closely concerned had had time to regain their sense of humour.

It happened that Mum and Dad had become friendly – an unusual friend I would have thought for them – with an elderly Professor of Mathematics at Aberdeen University and had invited him and his wife to dine at Tullochford. On the appointed day there were some anxious glances at the sky which looked as if snow threatened but not seriously enough to think of cancelling the arrangements. So they set off. That is to say the Professor and his wife set off from Aberdeen and Mum and Dad set off from Tullochford, for some reason being under the impression that it was the Professor who had invited them to dine with him. In the course of the twenty-mile journey in the pitch darkness it started to snow in earnest and by the time Mum and Dad arrived at the Professor's house even the city streets were ankle deep in slush. In the meantime the Professor and his wife had only managed to get to Tullochford by struggling through the last half-mile or so on foot through mounting snowdrifts, to be greeted by Adams, Dad's recently acquired butler, with the information that Captain and Mrs Sutherland were not at home and were not expecting any guests. To which Adams added by way of gratuitous information, that he understood them to be dining with Professor———in Aberdeen.

'But *I am* Professor———' he declared, understandably in a state of some agitation.

It was only by a stroke of the greatest good fortune that the telephone wires had not yet come down which was the inevitable consequence of any but the mildest of snow storms. Thus communication was established and it was agreed that any attempt to contend further with the forces of nature would be unwise and that they should each stay where they were for the night. Fortunately, too, the snow plough was able to get through the following morning otherwise they might have been unwitting guests for quite a few days in each others' houses.

Undoubtedly one of the most striking changes over the last sixty years has been the improvement in communications. It was for example inconceivable that the time would come when it would be possible to lift the telephone and dial any corner of the world and be instantly connected. To make a telephone call in those days, even locally, required a great deal of patience and not an inconsiderable amount of luck if you were to be connected to the number you required. There was no dialling system and the telephone exchanges were manually operated by the postmistress in the village who, in consequence, became the receptacle and the disseminator of all gossip. I can remember Mum was once talking on a trunk line when the line which had been quite clear suddenly became muffled whereupon the following exchange took place:

'I can't hear you very well, Hope.'

Mum: 'It'll be that old biddy at the post office listening in.'

Old Biddy: 'Ach, ye ken fine Missus Sutherland; I woulna' do a thing like thon!'

The telephone wires were of course carried above ground on telegraph poles spaced every thirty yards along the highways, each subscriber requiring two wires, one to send and one to receive. Inevitably any bad weather conditions resulted in wires coming down with all communications suspended, sometimes for days on end.

Add to this the unreliability of motor-cars and the poor condition of the roads and it will be realised that, at least in country districts, we were not much more advanced than in the days of the stage coach and the penny post of only fifty years earlier.

For us the Christmas holidays meant two things – one good, one bad. The bad thing was that, despite all the travelling difficulties, there were, year by year, an ever increasing number of Christmas parties for children of our age. There was a sort of understanding, amounting to a social commitment, entered into by our parents to the effect that if your brats came to our party, our brats must be asked to yours. Thus a dreadful social circuit was set up in a manner which can only be compared with the sort of thing which Society Ladies with eligible daughters still, I believe, contrive each year to set up on a rather larger stage and called The London Season. Except this was not London. It was hicks-in-the-sticks Aberdeenshire.

It was in fact our mother in collaboration with Jock Crawford's mother, Helena, who started the rot on only my second Christmas back from Alton Burn, much to the cringing horror of us all, which included Jock's younger brother Nigel, whose first term it was. They decided to give a vast joint Christmas party at Rothie Castle which was the only place vast enough to give such a shindig and for which purpose they opened up the old ballroom which had not been opened since the days of Queen Victoria. The whole thing drove the old Colonel to being a two-bottles-of-whisky-a-day man instead of the usual one. They even had a conjuror and after that Scottish dancing with lots of balloons and streamers and paper hats. The most extraordinary thing of all about this performance was that there were lots of girls present although where they came from none of us had the faintest idea nor, indeed who any of them were. All the families with whom we were on anything like intimate terms, such as the Gordons, the Leith-Hays or the Forbes' consisted entirely of boys. It could only be assumed that Helena Crawford and Mum were on intimate terms with some families which consisted only of girls; and this was subsequently to prove only too true. That party was only the thin edge of the wedge from which all manner of evils were to spring in the years to come.

It will be readily realised that the main, if not the only, objection to this socialising sprang from the amount of time it consumed at the expense of all the other things we had to fit in to our period away from school. The good thing was that, to add to our other sporting interests, Dad decided that the time had come when we were old enough to be allowed to shoot.

Just as the first steps to my lifelong love of fishing started when, at the age of six and three quarters, I first dropped a worm under the nose of a trout, so the transition from my first timid steps with a gun in my hand to when I could take a grouse screaming over my head at eighty miles an hour with the best of them, was a slow process.

My first gun was a ·410 with a single barrel whilst Gordon 'inherited' our mother's 20 bore which had two barrels and which I envied greatly. Incidently Mum was a very good game shot which, in those days, was unusual for a woman and, I suppose, still is.

Of course the whole shooting scene was very different from that of today. Whilst the lairds lucky enough to own a grouse moor were just beginning to grasp the commercial potential, it was by no means an easy matter to catch a tenant willing to rent it. It was quite unlike today when the queues of Dutch, French, Germans and Italians waving fistfuls of notes to book a place on the hillsides are very long indeed. In the 1920s and 30s almost the only customers were the Americans, all of whom, it was popularly believed, were millionaires. There was no question then of syndicating grouse moors and letting them out by the day, regardless of the prospects of a good bag. They were let for the whole season. The most careful records were kept and the only moors in with any chance of a profitable let were those in the top league.

By the same token the letting of salmon beats which today command such astronomical rents was far from an easy matter. It was the usual practice for an estate with a grouse moor and a stretch of salmon fishing to throw in the fishing with the moor. It was the custom with a party taking the shooting, for only the men to shoot and, whilst they were thus occupied, the womenfolk had to be content with spending their days by the river. This might explain why all the records of big catches and big fish are down to women. My mother was one of the very few of her sex who was allowed to take her place in the firing line on a grouse moor alongside the men.

At the same time there cannot be many boys today who can

spend every available day of their school holidays enjoying the delights of rough shooting in the way that we were able to do. At first our activities were restricted mainly to the pursuit of rabbits or waiting for pigeons flighting-in in the late winter afternoons to roost but very soon we we graduated to walking up partridges in the stubble fields or in the fields of turnips with the odd pheasant getting up from under one's feet as a bonus. Over at the back of Tullochford there was also a bog such as you used to find dotted over the countryside where snipe abounded and where from time to time mallard and teal would come into feed. Shooting too was something that many of our school friends not only enjoyed but had splendid opportunities of indulging. Rothie Castle was surrounded by woods where, with much expenditure of shot and shell, we could bag as many as a couple of dozen pigeons in a hard working day. There were other delights such as Knockespoke which belonged to 'Hag' and 'Lags' grandmother where pheasants abounded (they were comparatively rare on our ground) as well as the migratory woodcock. One day you could wander over the ground and not see a single bird; the next, particularly after a sharp frost or change in the weather, and the woods would be full of them.

Partridge shooting only opens on the first of September so that, with school term starting at the latest in mid-September, we had only a few days to enjoy it before being dragged off but as the Christmas holidays drew near all our talk at school was, not of the parties we might be going to or what we expected to find in our Christmas stockings but of days out with the gun.

In the grown-up world shooting was a way of life during the winter months. Everyone had shooting parties. Sometimes – in fact usually – they were just walking-up days and particularly on low ground such as ours where partridges were the main game. Only on the grander moors was the twelfth of August, the 'Glorious Twelfth' and the opening day of the grouse season, celebrated in grand style with a full turn out of beaters and birds driven over the guns. It was altogether a great day all round. From an hour or more before the guns took their place in the butts, the beaters would be out on the high tops, blanking in great expanses of moor in preparation for the first drive. When the whistle sounded to announce the moment for the line of beaters to start advancing from perhaps a mile away towards the line of guns you could feel a tension in the air equally as great as before the finalists step onto the Centre Court at Wimbledon or the Scottish Rugby team trot out of the tunnel at Murrayfield for their battle with the 'auld enemy', England. A beater would walk for upwards of twenty miles, struggling up crags or wading through deep heather in the course of a day's shooting be rewarded with half-a-crown at the end of it and with a bottle of beer to go with his sandwiches at lunch time but the competition to take part was keen indeed.

Lunch for the guns was often a very elaborate affair with white table cloths and glittering glass and cutlery laid out on tables in the shooting hut and such a spread of food and drink as to do credit to a *fête champêtre* in the gardens of the Palace of Versailles before the French Revolution. It was not the stuff, anyway sixty years ago, of which revolutions are made. There was much good-natured rivalry between estates and the sporting scene was part and parcel of the lives of everyone who worked as part of them. A good day on the hill was as much an occasion for general celebration as a bumper harvest or a top price at the cattle sales.

Of course these grand shooting affairs were then quite over our horizon although occasionally, as we got older, there were properly organised boys' shoots arranged as a sort of after New Year going-back-to-school present. Otherwise it was very much a matter for us of knocking round the hedges and ditches on our own and making the most of what each season had to offer with ferreting for rabbits or shooting vermin when game was out of season.

In these days of rampant commercialism, shooting has put on a rather different set of clothes. There is on one hand the unedifying spectacle of pheasants hand reared in their thousands being driven, if rumour does not lie, sometimes straight out of their rearing pens, to fly head high over the guns to satisfy the sporting aspirations of city businessmen;

on the other the great sporting estates have been given over to syndicates, mostly from our wealthier European neighbours, at unaffordably high prices. The day of the rough shoot has gone forever and with it part of the countryside has died.

As the winter term of 1930 approached a new menace showed above the horizon, at least so far as Gordon was concerned. Gordon's days at Alton Burn had never been happy. Most boys faced with the inevitability of boarding school eventually grow to accept it. Some even grow to like it. This Gordon never did. As N.G. reported on him after his first term, he never stopped looking out of the window to where the grass was always green, fish darted in their splashy pools and rabbits popped merrily in and out of their burrows. Thrash away as N.G. might, he preserved an air of studied indifference which even the mildest of his would-be mentors like Mr MacCarthy and Miss Brydon found frustrating.

He had now reached an age when Alton Burn had done what they could and it was required of another establishment that they should attempt the task of completing his educational curriculum.

The school decided upon was Trinity College, Glenalmond one of Scotland's four main Public Schools – the others being Fettes, Merchiston and Loretto. Glenalmond was not only the smallest but also the toughest. It was also the most remote being high up in the rugged Perthshire hills and six miles from the nearest village. Gordonstoun, where Prince Philip was to be sent, was not to be founded for another two years by Kurt Hahn, a refugee from Hitler's Jewish purges in Germany where he had pioneered a new type of educational system on the sound-in-mind, sound-in-body principle. There were also some revolutionary ideas about encouraging the pupils to sail boats, climb hills and generally embrace the outdoor life. Initially it drew many of its pupils from English schools and boys whose parents felt they were being misunderstood or that they were not fitted for the more conventional disciplines of Eton, Harrow, Rugby and the rest. Amongst Scottish Public

Schools, Gordonstoun was generally regarded as a very soft option indeed.

That winter term, Alton Burn took up a day later than Glenalmond. When it came for me to say goodbye to Gordon, we shook hands formally and I found myself wishing him luck but he had the look in his eye of someone who did not expect to come out of it alive.

CHAPTER ELEVEN

> This is not the end. It is not even the beginning of the end. But it is perhaps, the end of the beginning.
>
> Winston Churchill in a speech to the US Congress (24 December 1941)

My last year at Alton Burn before I was destined to join Gordon at Glenalmond was for me what one might call a piece of cake. As I had gone there at a rather more tender age than most, my closest friends had been more Gordon's age and left at the same time as him. Some, like Rodney Hitchcock, were also going to Glenalmond whilst others, for example Jock Crawford and the Gordon brothers, to a variety of other schools, some even to England, where Sedbergh in the Lake District was a popular choice. This rather left me as cock of the roost and I became Head Boy and Captain of Games and a figure of some authority amongst the younger boys.

In the years when I had been there Alton Burn had in fact rather grown in size, although not yet above twenty-five boys so my honours may not have been as hard-earned as they sounded. There had also been one or two colourful additions to our ranks. There was Erland Clouston, a fellow Orcadian, whose father Storer Clouston's reputation as a novelist, at that time, rivalled even that of Eric Linklater, yet another of Orkney's famous sons in the literary tradition. Then, too there was Alasdair Gordon whose father Seton Gordon was the almost legendary naturalist and writer who lived on the island of Skye and devoted a lifetime to the study of the golden eagle. He used to come and stay at Alton Burn, often for several days at the time. We were never left long in doubt of his arrival for he would greet each crack of dawn by marching up and down on the front lawn, in full Highland dress, blowing the bagpipes. I do not know whether it was from an early addiction to the pipes or from some other cause but he was almost totally deaf, an affliction which did not preclude his being recognised as a leading authority and judge of pipe music throughout Scotland. He was also a pioneer of bird photography and the slide-lantern lectures he gave to the school still stick vividly in my memory.

There was another boy who was something of a mystery and who became a great friend of mine. His name was Felix de Hamel and his grandmother lived in a large mansion, called Alton Don, which stood up on a hill overlooking the school. His mother and, I think, an aunt were also there most of the time and he had a pony-mad sister called Yvonne. Although Felix boarded at the school like everyone else he was allowed to spend Sunday, after church service, at Alton Don and quite often I was allowed to go as well. The house was filled with heavy Oriental furniture, Turkish carpets and hanging drapes which gave it an air of mystery. Felix was a delightful companion who, rather to my alarm, declared in the course of my last term that it was his intention to become a missionary. As any form of religious zeal was totally unknown in the school, this took me considerably by surprise. Nor do I know if he ever achieved his ambition. He went off to school somewhere in England and, although I went to stay with the family once or twice after that, I eventually lost touch. During the war I was surprised to learn that he had been taken prisoner of war and, on account of a close family relationship with Winston Churchill, had been interned at Colditz Castle along with other politically-sensitive prisoners. And there the mystery rests. By and large school boys, even living in the enforced intimacy of a boarding school, are incurious about each others' backgrounds and only concerned whether they think them good chaps or not.

Another unexpected arrival in our midst was a Russian boy

called Alexis Wrangel. His father, Baron Wrangel, had been one of the most dashing generals in the Russian army. He had been a member of the Russian Imperial Guard and in the war had commanded the Cossacks, surely the most glamorous troops of the Czar's army. After the February Revolution he remained loyal to the Tsarist regime and eventually commanded the White (anti-Bolshevik) Army. I think the General must have died a year or so before Alexis came to Alton Burn and he was accompanied by his mother, a Belgian Baroness in her own right and of formidable appearance. Alexis had spent most of his young life in Belgium so how he came to find himself in this tiny school in the north of Scotland and surrounded by a bunch of boys who had only the very foggiest idea of what happened south of Edinburgh, it is very hard to imagine. He was a delicate-looking boy with a narrow aristocratic face and fair curly hair. He had an amazingly precocious skill with a pencil and produced wonderfully funny sketches, particularly of N.G., which would have earned him six of the best had they fallen into the hands of his model. Far from lapsing into moods of deep gloom, which is popularly considered to be in the nature of all Russians, he was always as merry as a cricket and into every rough and tumble going.

That last summer remains in my memory as a particularly golden one. Senior boys were allowed certain privileges which included outings with Mr MacCarthy who took us bird-watching out on the great expanses of the Culbin Sands or trips on one of the fishing boats working out of the then still-thriving fishing port of Nairn. Treats organised by N.G. were predictably of a rather more military nature such as being taken to watch the Seaforth Highlanders beating Retreat at their Headquarter Barracks at Fort George. The Seaforth Highlanders were, in N.G.'s opinion, one of the finest regiments in the whole British Army, and it was the proper ambition for any boy who might, for any reason, be unable to get into the Gordon Highlanders, to try to take a commission. That any boy who was not, by reason of primogeniture, due to inherit a large estate should do anything else with his life other than join the army was something which simply did not cross his mind.

N.G.'s other favourite excursion was to view the site of the Battle of Culloden, the bleak moor above Inverness where the ragged and half-starved remnants of Bonnie Prince Charlie's army hurled themselves in one last desperate charge onto the bayonets of Butcher Cumberland's men and which ended the uprising of 1745. We would all stand in silence whilst he pointed out the barrows of earth which marked the mass graves of each clan. 'That's your family, Macdonald' he would say. 'And this is yours, Macintosh. Your lot are a bit further over there, Cameron.'

Then, as a cue for giving an impromptu lesson on the works of Robert Louis Stevenson, he would recite:

> Blows the wind today and the sun and the rain are flying,
> Blows the wind on the moors today and now,
> Where about the graves of the martyrs the whaups are crying,
> My heart remembers how!
> Be it granted me to behold you again in dying,
> To hear once more the peewee's cry
> And then to hear no more.

I have always thought that, had he been given the opportunity, N.G. could have given a performance as Shakespeare's *Macbeth* to have rivalled the greatest actors of all time.

At the end of the summer term it had been decided that, instead of taking the Common Entrance examination, I should sit for a scholarship. This meant that I was given the dignity of a small room at the top of the main staircase as my own where I could do some swotting. This was something of which N.G. was quick to take advantage by giving me also the intake of new boys to instruct in the first steps in Latin. However, despite this not too onerous task, I managed to win an Exhibitioner Scholarship to Glenalmond.

CHAPTER TWELVE

FLOREAT GLENALMOND, GLENALMOND FLOREAT

New boys in their first term at Glenalmond were required to arrive a day before the rest of the school. They did not report to their assigned House but to the Probationer House – 'Pro. House' – where they spent their first term removed from the hurly-burly of life in the Junior Common Room. This humane arrangement had several advantages which included exemption from cold baths, their own locker room to change in for games and, above all, no house prefects.

On the other hand, no sooner had one been shown one's allotted bed-space in the dormitory and with hardly time to start unpacking, than a summons to the House Master's study was received. He was a kindly, slightly old-womanish bachelor, much given to favourites and with only the tiniest hint of sadism behind his highly-polished glasses – and the first thing he did was to hand each apprehensive boy a copy of the school song *Carmen Glenalmonense* with instructions that it was to be learnt by heart, initially only verses one, two and five, and to be ready to be examined on it in three days' time. It was a formidable task by any standards and particularly for any new boy who may not have had the advantage of N.G.'s ferocious grounding in Latin.

Nor was this the only task to be undertaken in one's spare time in those first three days. It was also required that a thorough knowledge be acquired of the school geography, including distant corners of the extensive grounds. Thus not to be able to come up with the answer to such questions as 'Where is Snipe Corner?' 'What and where is the Lantern?'

or 'Where is Big Hole and what is it used for?' would result in immediate and condign punishment to be administered by the examiner who would be a House Prefect of the House which one was down to join.

The disciplinary hierarchy at Glenalmond was, of necessity, far more elaborate than at Alton Burn where N.G. was the single arbiter. At Glenalmond there was a four-tier system. The lowest forum of physical punishment was the House Prefects who dealt with internal trangressions such as noisy ragging in the Junior Common Room, dodging the morning cold bath, talking in the dorm after lights out and so on. On the next layer were the School Prefects – 'Beaks' in Glenalmondese – who dealt with offenders against the school's own rules of behaviour and these were legion and complex. Probably the most cardinal sin was for someone who was not a prefect to walk on the beautifully-mown grass in the Quad – the quadrangle around which the school buildings were arranged with the Library set in the middle. There were however other offences of almost equal gravity. To be caught with one's hands in one's pockets or to have the wrong number of buttons undone on a jacket were certain ways of earning a beating. The number of buttons allowed to be left undone was of great importance and related to which grade of class you were in. Boys in the most junior classes had to keep all three buttons done up at all times. Once in the Fifth however things became more relaxed and the top button could be undone; in the Sixth Form the top two were permissable but only Prefects had the privilege of having all buttons undone and of swaggering around with their jackets open and both hands deep in their trouser pockets. To run past such a great personage was an offence; the moment one hove into view one had to slow down to a walk and, of course, to leave any of one's possessions about, such as a dropped gym shoe in a cloister, was to invite swift retribution.

Next grade up in the whacking order were the Form Masters whose jurisdiction was over inattentiveness in class or anti-social behaviour like flicking ink pellets or prodding the boy at the next desk with your compass. In this grade also came your House Master who had special powers to intervene with a rather higher class of whacking for more serious offences. Finally, and most awesome of all, there was the Headmaster himself who was referred to by all as the 'Grue'. I have no idea how this name, reaching back into history, came about. Could it have been an abbreviation by some boy in the last century for 'gruesome'?

The Headmaster when I first went to Glenalmond was Canon Matheson, the last in a line of High Churchmen to hold the office, reaching back to the foundation of the School by the Prime Minister William Ewart Gladstone who, by way of a reward, had a cloister named after him as well as one of the more distant playing fields. Canon Matheson was an impressive figure. Very tall and dignified with woolly white hair, he was usually to be sighted stalking round the quad, deep in thought and puffing at an enormous cigar. It was said that the only time he did not have a cigar in his mouth was when he was asleep or in church. Even the school reports sent to parents in the middle of the holidays reeked of cigar smoke. He was a life-long bachelor whose maiden sister kept house for him and whose brother acted as Bursar for the College. He dispensed justice with a strong right arm and rewarded virtue with a paternal pat on the head. All in all he was a jolly good Headmaster.

Unlike the stark Presbyterian preachings to which we had been subjected at Alton Burn, Glenalmond was about as High Church as you could get short of Catholicism. The day started at seven in the morning with the tolling of the five-minute bell for Chapel and the end of the school day was marked with evening service at six o'clock. After that there were only two hours of prep and a mug of cocoa with bread and margarine to be got through before bed.

There were however certain concessions which came with the process of growing up and going off to public school, which may not seem to be exactly epoch-making in the eyes of more modern generations but which marked quite a milestone in our lives.

One of the things was that going to Glenalmond brought with it the privilege of wearing our first long trousers. No boys in those days ever wore long trousers until they were approaching their teens. Looking back now, when to see a boy in short trousers is a thing of the past, this seems strange, particularly in view of the often arctic conditions we had to endure but that was the custom of those times. Even then long grey flannels were only for best and most of the time we continued to wear corduroy shorts with a sweater and open-necked shirt.

Another thing was that at the beginning of each term we were given pocket money by our parents which on arrival at school had to be handed over immediately to our house master. It was forbidden for boys to keep money on their person or in their lockers. It was also limited to three pounds but that represented an enormous sum in those days. It was issued out to each boy each week to spend in the school tuck shop and represented about half a crown each week. It was quite within a boy's right, should he wish to live recklessly, to draw as heavily as he liked on his bank but when it was gone it was gone and no anguished letters to parents were of any avail. When one considers that some of the boys were sixteen or seventeen years old this must seem faintly ridiculous but, on the other hand, there was simply nothing to spend it on except making a pig of one's self over tuck.

Then there were the tuck boxes, the contents of which were the subject of much agonising. The contents had to last a whole term so large cakes were not a good idea as they went stale. The main aim was to supplement the evening diet of cocoa and bread and marg. so that one of the most sensible investments were things like small tins of Nestlé's condensed milk which could be consumed in one go and sent one happily to bed. All in all it made for a good grounding in prudent husbandry.

During my first term when I was isolated in Pro House I did not see a great deal of Gordon during the week but at weekends we were allowed 'dockets'. This entailed applying to your house master to be out of school from eleven o'clock in the morning until six o'clock Chapel in the evening. On the application you had to state which boy or boys you were going with and exactly where you were going. The options in this latter respect were rather limited as it had to be within walking distance which meant if you wanted to keep to the low ground either up or down the River Almond or, for the more adventurous, straight up the side of a mountain.

I really believe that Gordon, who had resolutely remained in the 'Shell' (the name given to the bottom class) ever since his arrival, spent his whole week planning for these dockets. We were allowed to draw sandwiches from the dining hall after breakfast and we supplemented this with various things such as chocolate bars and biscuits as well as a large bottle each of some fizzy drink. It was almost always Rodney Hitchcock, Gordon and I who made up our party and the planning of the commissariat, so that we did not all buy the same goodies, was of critical importance. This caused Gordon agonies of planning and much scribbling of little notes to Rodney and me when concealed behind the raised lid of his desk during some lesson, the importance of which was dwarfed by comparison with the business in hand. But for Gordon, and indeed for all three of us, this was not the half.

Hidden up in the folds in the hills and below the high corries there were deep, rush-encircled, tarns which, with a hatch of flies, boiled with trout. And not, as in lots of Scottish hill lochs, were they undersized little trout starved by being too many for too little feeding, but big trout of a pound or more which made deep rings on the surface of the water when they rose to a fly. I do not suppose there can be many schools where fishing rods are an acceptable addition to the bare necessities permitted but Glenalmond was, and I hope still is, one of them.

There were, so far as I can remember, only three days in each term when visits by parents were permitted of which by far the most important was half-term when boys could be taken out on both Saturday and Sunday. As the school was so remote, to take their boys out must have presented parents who lived down in England, of which there were quite a few, problems of nightmare proportions. There was really no accommodation within a radius of twenty miles and little to do with the little beasts when they got them. In this we were very lucky as Granny at Kinloch was only some thirty miles away and served as an admirable base for Mum and Dad who would otherwise have been faced with a round journey of over two hundred miles.

In the same way as there had been at Alton Burn, there was always a considerable show of interest amongst all the boys in other boys' parents and particularly in what sort of conveyance they turned up in. I do not think that this had any basis in an innate snobbishness but rather was a subject for good-natured ragging. Certainly parents had no chance at all of avoiding the stares from a highly critical auditorium. All visitors had to pass through the tunnel which constituted the lodge gateway into the quad to park under the windows of all the boys anxiously waiting their arrival.

'Oh, come quick, Carruthers! Your Dad's come to take you out!' some humourist would be sure to shout as the refuse collection lorry rumbled into the quad.

Perhaps, on consideration, there was with some boys a certain amount of one-upmanship in the whole thing. I remember on one visiting day instead of Mum and Dad trundling up in Dad's modest Austin, Mum arrived instead with Sandy Irvine who drove a very rakish, open Aston Martin with Brooklands Racing Club badges lined up on the front bumper, with the vroom! vroom! of the engine as he revved it rather flamboyantly echoing round the quad. After that quite a few senior boys who might not have done so otherwise condescended to talk to Gordon and me.

To belong to the OTC (Officers' Training Corps) was obligatory and infuriatingly it interfered with the docket system in the summer term whilst we clambered up and down mountains, stormed imaginary strong points and held field days which always happened at our precious weekends and, in the winter, much time was spent in training for the inter-house cross-country run. This was a frantically strenuous race of six miles over the roughest and most precipitous country they could find. 'Bratter' Gordon, cured of his incontinence but still beaten, on one pretext or another at least once a week, caused quite a stir by winning the Junior in his first term. I only mention this so that I can slip in the fact that I won it on my second year. A greater feat in my opinion even than getting one's first fifteen colours.

All in all for a boy to arrive for his first term at any public school, however benign, is a chastening experience. For a boy who had not previously been a boarder at a preparatory school it must be traumatic. For all, as they become senior in their previous educational establishment and begin to assume the dignity of their teenage years, it virtually means starting all over again. To be at one moment cock of the walk, strutting one's superiority amongst one's admiring juniors and the next to be amongst the lowest of the low, required at the cry of 'fag!' or the snap of an older boy's fingers to come running, is a chastening experience and very good for the soul. I suppose that the exceptional rigours of life at Glenalmond were better for the soul than most, at least if the fine records of many of my contemporary *alumni montium* and succeeding generations of O.G.s are anything to go by.

Looking back now to my Glenalmond schooldays, it does seem extraordinary how everyone accepted the disciplines and punishments, fair or unfair, with such equanimity and even more extraordinary how it generated a spirit of loyalty and fierce pride amongst us. At the end of term when the Carmen was sung in full on Speech Day and it came to the final O FLOREAT GLENALMOND, GLENALMOND FLOREAT the lung-bursting crescendo was impressive in its fervour – but then, of course, that could have been from a relief in the knowledge that we would all be going home the next day for the holidays.

CHAPTER THIRTEEN

O! that a man might know
The end of this day's business ere it come.
Julius Caesar William Shakespeare

It was not only at Glenalmond that the growing-up process was forced upon us so inexorably. More and more during the holidays we found ourselves involved in all manner of activities far removed from the early halcyon years when everything which went on at the farm had absorbed us so completely. Now it was turning into a battle with our parents to get any time to play on our own cabbage patch.

I remember coming back for one Christmas holidays to find that there had been some sort of party arranged for almost every day until we had to go back to school. Worse, the parties were not any longer simple affairs with lots of ice-cream, orange squash and paper streamers. They were the sort of parties we had to dress up for in full party plumage; black kilt jacket with silver buttons, elaborate cravat, dress sporran and with a *skean dhu* stuck in the stocking top; and we were expected to dance with girls. Not just the odd Highland Fling but foxtrots and waltzes with one arm round their middles and the other holding your partner's high in the air like a sail. The worst part about these affairs was that they took part mostly in the afternoons which meant, if the party was any distance away, getting all togged up in time for an early lunch before the off, and that was really a whole day wasted when we could have been out doing all the things we had been planning and looking forward to for most of the school term.

There was another form of entertainment which, when we

were well into our teens, was creeping up upon us. It was called a Picnic Dance and was very much *à la mode* in Aberdeenshire social circles in the 1930s. I imagine it evolved from the fact that everyone still lived in far too large houses with far too little money and with the post-war crop of teenagers whom parents felt they ought to 'do something for' in the holidays. The formula, which was actually rather a good one, was this. Invitations were sent out to bring a party of your own equipped with sufficient food and drink for whoever you brought. Thus someone with a houseful of guests could bring them or invite others to make up their party. All the drink went into a common pool and your party picnicked at the table reserved for it round the ballroom floor or wherever space permitted and the hostess provided the rest such as the band and waiters as well as setting up a bar where you simply went and ordered whatever you were drinking. The wise hostess also laid in a reserve (on sale or return) of every kind of drink. The most shaming thing which could happen was for the drink to run out and these affairs were apt to go on well into the small hours of the morning. In fact so anxious were the guests not to appear mean that they always brought far more than their party could possibly consume so that whoever hosted the party generally found themselves with enough leftovers to keep them going for several months afterwards.

It was also very much not done for anyone to bring an inferior wine and particularly a less than top-rate champagne. Nothing could spell social death more certainly than to be identified as trying to sneak in an inferior brand which might find its way onto someone else's table. The same considerations applied to the food you provided for your party. To have your table loaded with ham sandwiches and potato crisps when all the others were groaning under lobster, cold salmon and sides of beef was to invite a certain amount of whispering behind hands. Besides which everyone was expected to go table-hopping both to find other dancing partners and tuck into whatever they had to offer in the way of delicacies.

Predictably Gordon simply could not stand these affairs and

would usually try and slip away to hide in the gardens lest anyone should seek to drag him onto the dance floor. I being of a rather more extrovert nature began to find that I was actually enjoying myself and somehow feeling faintly guilty about doing so.

One compensating by-product of our parents' extremely active social life was that our invitations to fish at places like Drum Castle and Tilliefourie did not dry up. In fact if anything they became even more frequent. It was at this time that Dad started to get his headaches badly. He had suffered from them for as long as I could remember but now they became much more severe and frequent. He made no conessions to these bouts like lying down in a darkened room; nor so far as I know did he ever resort to taking analgesics. They were the symptoms of an illness which was eventually to kill him.

I suppose most children, absorbed in their own affairs, are to a degree insensitive to what is going on around them. Perhaps Gordon and I were more insensitive than most. Our parents never quarrelled, or certainly not in front of us. Indeed they always seemed most amiable towards one another but they were growing apart.

They seldom went to the same places together. It was for instance always with Mum that we went to Drum and always with Dad that we went to spend the day at Tilliefourie.

Then one day it happened. Gordon and I were mucking about down by the stables one morning when word was sent down from the house that our father wanted to see us in what was rather over-grandly called the library.

Dad in his plus-fours, his hands deep in his pockets, was standing in front of the fireplace. Mum was over by the window, gazing out over the rockwall.

'Your mother and I have decided that we are to go our different ways' he harrumphed, spreading his feet widely apart. 'Your mother is to go to your grandmother at Kinloch. Your brother, John will go with her. I shall, of course, stay here. You must decide what you want to do. Stay here or go with your mother. We want to know now. Gordon first.'

Gordon stood for what seemed like hours, his eyes fixed on the blue sky out of the window. Finally he said:

'I'll stay here.'

'And you, Douglas?' asked Father.

'I'll stay with Gordon' I said.

And that was how it ended. My childhood was suddenly over. Not with a bang but a whimper.